Raising Joyful Lifelong Learners

Raising Joyful Lifelong Learners

How to Support Children's
Natural Learning Processes

Aletha J. Solter, PH.D.

SHINING STAR PRESS ✷ GOLETA, CALIFORNIA

Published by Shining Star Press
Post Office Box 206
Goleta, California 93116, U.S.A.
Phone & Fax: (805) 968–1868
Email: info@awareparenting.com
Website: www.awareparenting.com (The Aware Parenting Institute)

Book design: Studio E Books, Santa Barbara
Cover photo credit: iStock.com/RuslanGuzov

First printing 2025

PUBLISHER'S CATALOGING INFORMATION
Solter, Aletha Jauch, 1945–
Raising joyful lifelong learners: how to support children's natural learning processes / Aletha J. Solter
Includes bibliographical references.
ISBN: 979-8-9865429-4-2
1. Child psychology. 2. Child rearing. 3. Educational psychology. 4. Learning, Psychology of. I. Title.
Dewey Decimal Classification: 649.1
Library of Congress Control Number: 2025907861

This book is dedicated to my parents, who gave me the freedom to play and explore my interests, to the many wonderful teachers who inspired me, to my children, who have taught me so much about the learning process, and to my husband, who has supported me on my lifelong learning journey.

Acknowledgments

I would like to express my appreciation to the following people who read the manuscript and gave me constructive feedback: my husband, Ken Solter; my son, Nicholas Solter; and my daughter, Sarah Solter. I am also grateful to my son and his children, who allowed me to interview them for this book, and to the following Aware Parenting instructors who shared their personal experiences: Christoph Geiger (Germany), Joss Goulden (Australia), Rico Heinisch (Germany), Marion Rose, Ph.D. (Australia), Françoise Somers (Belgium), Corinne Sprecher (Switzerland), Nathalie Trudel (China), and Vivian Viester (Switzerland). Finally, I would like to acknowledge the researchers and educational reformers from many countries whose work has inspired me.

Contents

List of Charts

Warning/Disclaimer

As an educational resource for parents, this book offers information about approaches to education based on children's natural learning processes. These suggestions may not be appropriate for children suffering from certain physical, neurological, developmental, emotional, or behavioral problems. This book is not intended to replace professional educational advice, diagnoses, psychotherapy, or medical care from competent professionals. If your child is struggling to learn, it is advisable to obtain professional advice and treatment.

The mention of specific educational approaches in this book is for informational purposes only and does not constitute an endorsement by the author. If you are looking for a school for your child, it is important to visit the school, fully understand its teaching and discipline approach, and carefully review the teachers' credentials.

The author and publisher make no guarantees regarding the effectiveness of the suggestions in this book, and they shall have neither liability nor responsibility to any person or entity with respect to any damage caused, or alleged to be caused, directly or indirectly by the information contained in this book.

Raising Joyful Lifelong Learners

Introduction

THIS BOOK describes children's natural learning processes and the best teaching practices to support their learning from birth to age twelve. I wrote it primarily for parents, but teachers will also find the information relevant. Both parents and teachers play a vital role in educating children and shaping their attitudes toward learning.

I question many cultural assumptions about learning, which manifest in outdated and ineffective teaching methods. Some teaching practices cause stress for children, and some can even be harmful. I am not placing blame on teachers, who often have little freedom or training to implement approaches that differ from those mandated by educational institutions. My goal is to highlight educational practices that are ineffective, stressful, or even damaging, regardless of how loving and well-intentioned parents and teachers may be.

If you experienced ineffective or harmful teaching methods as a child, you may have a clear idea of what to avoid when raising your own children. However, you might struggle to envision alternative approaches that are both effective and nurturing. This book provides numerous examples of teaching strategies that foster learning without compromising children's motivation or self-confidence. I have also included guidelines to help children recover from stressful or traumatic learning experiences at school, at home, or elsewhere. With emotional support, children can heal and regain their eagerness to learn.

The learning approach described in this book is part of a parenting approach I call Aware Parenting. My other books explore various aspects of this approach, which consists of three key components: attachment-based parenting, nonpunitive discipline, and tools for helping children recover from stress and trauma. Although you don't need to read my other books to benefit from this one, familiarity with the Aware Parenting approach may help you implement some of the suggestions more easily. Certified instructors in over 25 countries offer Aware Parenting workshops, consultations, and support groups.

I have identified twelve principles of learning, some of which are not widely recognized, that can guide and support children's education. A large body of research in psychology, education, and child development supports these principles. In my first draft of this book, I summarized the twelve principles of learning in one of the first chapters. While revising it, however, I realized that this book itself is a form of teaching and that it might be useful for it to be structured in alignment with the principles of learning, one of which is learning by discovery. I therefore rearranged the order of the chapters to encourage readers to discover the principles of learning before I explicitly describe them. Several of the first chapters include examples and experiences (including my own), with the goal of inspiring readers to think about the learning process, especially those who have not previously encountered some of these ideas.

I have had unique learning and teaching experiences. By sharing my personal experiences, I illustrate my own journey of discovery, specifically how I gained insight into the learning process. In addition to my own experiences, I have included those of my children and grandchildren, whom I interviewed for this book. Several Aware Parenting instructors (including some who are teachers) have also contributed their personal examples and experiences. With their permission, I have used their real names.

The principles of learning are summarized in Chapter 8, by which point readers will already have a basic understanding of them from reading the previous chapters. I realize that my approach of illustrating the principles before explicitly explaining them may not appeal to everybody, so please feel free to read Chapter 8 first if you would like an immediate overview of the principles of learning. You can also find them on the Aware Parenting Institute website at the following link: http://www.awareparenting.com/learning.htm. The reference section at the back of the book provides supporting studies.

The following chart summarizes the basic assumptions and themes of this book.

Basic assumptions and themes

1. Children are born with an innate desire and ability to learn. They are naturally curious, and their brains automatically absorb information while striving to make sense of their experiences.

2. Twelve fundamental principles of learning align with children's natural learning processes. These principles, supported by research, apply to all children.

3. Educational approaches that honor these principles foster deep, meaningful learning. In such environments, children feel engaged and enjoy the learning process.

4. Educational approaches that deviate from these principles can hinder children's motivation and ability to learn. Such environments can cause stress, frustration, confusion, anxiety, anger, or low self-confidence, making learning an unpleasant experience.

5. Children can recover from harmful teaching methods and regain their innate motivation and ability to learn.

By following the guidelines in this book, your children can learn and thrive, whether you teach them at home or they attend a public or private school. Please remember that your situation is unique, and your application of this information will be shaped by your own experiences and the children in your life. If you carry emotional wounds from your own stressful school experiences, your child's painful experiences may trigger long-buried memories of your childhood. If this happens, the exercises at the end of this book can help you identify the root causes of your emotions and heal from those stressful learning experiences.

You can support your children's learning effectively regardless of your financial situation, education level, or teaching experience. I hope this book provides you with ideas and inspiration to help your children become confident, joyful, and lifelong learners.

My Experiences with Schools, Learning, and Teaching

> *"Education is not preparation for life;*
> *education is life itself."*
> —*John Dewey*

MY IDEAS ABOUT teaching and learning have been influenced by my personal experiences. In this chapter, I describe the schools I attended as a child, teenager, and young adult in three countries. I also share my teaching experiences, which have further shaped my understanding of the learning process. In the final section, I describe my children's school experiences.

My school and learning experiences
Birth to age twelve
I had an unusual educational journey. I was born in the United States and lived there until the age of twelve. However, my first experience with formal schooling was in Cambridge, England, where we spent a year when I was four years old. My father, a physics professor, worked for one year as a visiting Fulbright Scholar at Cambridge University.

In Cambridge, my two older siblings and I attended a public (government-funded) school for children aged four to eight. As part of the British "infant school" system, it offered a child-centered, play-based environment, which also included some periods of direct instruction. In addition to free play and many craft activities, I was taught to read, write, and do simple addition problems. I enjoyed that school and had no trouble learning what was taught. By the time I returned to the United States at the age of five, I had a perfect British accent!

In the United States, we lived in Iowa, where my parents enrolled us in a progressive school associated with the university's education department. I attended that school until I was twelve and a half. I had no homework or tests until the age of twelve, and my teachers did not evaluate me with grades. Instead, they sent written comments about my progress to my parents twice a year.

I loved that school. My favorite teacher, a young man in his twenties, taught sixth grade (age eleven). We learned about vision and optics by making cardboard cameras, which actually worked! We took pictures with our homemade cameras, developed the film, and printed the photos in the school's darkroom. Our teacher arranged for a store in our town to display some of our photographs in its window. He asked for volunteers to write short essays to accompany the photographs explaining how we had made the cameras, developed the film, and printed the pictures. I volunteered to write an essay, which I wrote using my very best handwriting. For weeks afterward, I loved seeing our essays and photographs in the store window as I walked past on my way home from school.

That year, we also studied Mexico, and our teacher started by asking us what we wanted to learn about the country. He gave us the opportunity to ask as many questions as we wanted, and he wrote all our questions on the blackboard. We each copied the questions and chose which ones to research using books from the school library. I was particularly interested in learning what kinds of games the children in Mexico played. After researching our questions, we shared what we had learned with the rest of the class.

As a final activity, our class wrote a play about Mexico and performed it for our parents and the other children in the school. Our play began with a young girl encountering a magic genie in her bedroom, who took her on an imaginary trip back in time to observe scenes from three different periods of Mexican history. (I loved playing the role of the genie!) For the Aztec period, we made sure to include a scene depicting human sacrifice!

That year, we also visited an art museum to view a travelling exhibit of small Dutch Renaissance paintings. Our teacher asked us to choose a painting we liked and write a short paragraph describing our feelings about it. I enjoyed writing about my feelings while looking at a painting by Rembrandt.

Age twelve to age eighteen

When I was twelve years old, we moved to Europe, and I felt very sad to leave the progressive school in the United States. During my first year in Europe, we lived in Geneva, in the French-speaking part of Switzerland. I attended a private English-language international school, where I had my first French class. The following year, my father's work took us to London, England, for a year, where I attended a private bilingual (English/French) school.

At the bilingual school in London, I had some classes in English and some in French, and I experienced my first academic failure. I was enrolled in a French class for native speakers (after having studied the language for only one year). In that class, we had to write essays in French.

The French language is difficult to spell because it contains many silent letters. Furthermore, correct spelling requires an understanding of its grammatical structure. Spelling is typically evaluated by dictation tests, in which the teacher slowly reads a paragraph aloud, and the students write it down. In my first dictation test at that school, I did not understand the sentences and had no idea how to spell the words. I did the best I could, writing phonetically, which doesn't work very well in French! Not surprisingly, my paragraph had over fifty errors, and I received a failing grade. I felt that I shouldn't have been graded at all since I was not a native French speaker.

The following year, when I was fourteen, we settled permanently in Geneva, Switzerland, where my father became the director of the theoretical physics department at the university. My parents enrolled me in the academic (university-track) public high school, where all subjects were taught in French. Through full immersion, I soon became fluent. Since I enjoyed learning languages, I chose a course of study that included the other official languages of Switzerland (German and Italian).

One of my favorite teachers taught German language and literature. By my final year before graduation, we had mastered German grammar and had begun studying literature. During that year, our teacher immersed us in the German language for several weeks by narrating the long story told in a famous German epic poem from the Middle Ages (*Das Nibelungenlied*). He knew the plot by heart and entertained us daily with ten-minute segments. I was captivated by the story, which was filled with themes of love and betrayal. He often stopped at a suspenseful moment, leaving me eager to hear more the next day. This approach reinforced and increased my knowledge of German grammar and vocabulary without relying on direct instruction, memorization, drills, or tests. It was one of my most enjoyable learning experiences at that school.

The most stressful aspect of that school was the large amount of homework, with a strong emphasis on memorization. We had both scheduled tests and surprise quizzes. We received grades and were rank ordered each year from best to worst based on our grade point average. To make matters worse, the entire student list, in order from best to worst, was published in Geneva's main newspaper at the end of each school year! Terrified of failure, I often studied more than necessary to ensure that I would receive a good grade. My parents did not pressure me, but my own anxiety and internal drive to excel caused me to put pressure on myself.

By the time I graduated at the age of eighteen, I had been exposed to all the basic sciences, as well as history, geography, and mathematics (including calculus). I was also fluent in four languages and had read the main literary works in those languages. I felt proud when I passed the final exams required for university entry.

Age eighteen to age twenty-three

When I enrolled in the University of Geneva, I chose a program leading to a master's degree in human biology. The first two years consisted of courses with the medical students, including lectures and labs in the basic sciences (botany, zoology, chemistry, and physics), as well as human physiology and anatomy (which included human dissection). The program also required courses in anthropology, genetics, evolution, and psychology, including Jean Piaget's two-year course in development psychology and his advanced seminars.

Piaget's classes sparked my interest in how children learn. I loved knowing that he had based his theories on careful observations of his own children, and I enjoyed his emphasis on the development of children's thought processes. At the time, I did not realize that he was famous.

Most of the final exams were oral ones, requiring a private meeting with the professors, who asked any questions they wanted. Unfortunately, I failed my oral physics exam at the end of my first year. The professor asked me to explain how a Geiger counter worked. I didn't know the answer and had no memory of learning that in his class. Then he asked me to estimate the amount of water vapor in the room. I had no idea how to do that.

Giving me one last chance to demonstrate some knowledge of physics, he asked me to explain how the water vapor in the room could be measured. By that time, I could barely think, and I mumbled that I didn't know. I had spent weeks studying and memorizing basic physics principles and formulas, from mechanics to electromagnetic radiation, but he didn't ask me about anything that I had studied.

My failure on that exam was a serious blow to my self-esteem, and I also felt very embarrassed, because my father was a professor in that same physics department! I didn't have much experience with failure, and I began to doubt that I was smart enough to earn a university degree. Luckily, I had a second chance to pass the exam, so I tried again in the fall. That time, the professor asked me a question about the structure of atoms, and I knew enough to receive a passing grade.

After that humbling experience, I bravely continued my studies and eventually passed all my required exams, including written and oral exams with Professor Piaget. After five years, I earned a master's degree in human biology and decided to pursue a doctoral degree in psychology in the United States. With a letter of recommendation from Piaget, I was easily accepted into the Ph.D. program at the University of California.

My music education

My parents exposed me to music at an early age by introducing me to classical music and singing together around the piano. My siblings and I sang in a children's choir, where we were taught to sing in harmony. My father, an accomplished amateur violinist, enjoyed playing in a string quartet, which often met in our home. He was also the concertmaster (first-chair violinist) in the university orchestra, and I enjoyed attending his concerts.

Because of his deep interest in music, my father dreamed of creating a family string quartet. He wanted my brother to play the cello and hoped that my sister and I would learn to play the violin. To complete the quartet, he planned to play the viola part. To reach his goal, he arranged for my brother to take cello lessons, and he gave violin lessons to my sister and me. When I was eight years old, we began weekly lessons with him, and he even bought us brand-new, child-sized violins.

Unfortunately, my father's plan did not work. My brother did not enjoy playing the cello and soon refused to continue, but my father still hoped that my sister and I would learn to play the violin. However, he had not asked me if I wanted to play that instrument, and I had no desire to do so. Nevertheless, I dutifully followed his instructions and practiced daily, but I did not enjoy it. Learning from him was not a pleasant experience.

His teaching style upset me because he often lost patience when we played out of tune. My sister and I would go to our mother in tears, saying, "Daddy yelled at us again." My mother did her best to console us, explaining that our father had "sensitive ears" and found it hard to listen to off-key notes. I angrily replied that he shouldn't be giving violin lessons if he had such sensitive ears!

When I was ten years old, I started teaching myself to play simple tunes on the piano. My brother, who was three years older, had started taking piano lessons by then, and he helped me learn some of the pieces he was studying. Seeing me spontaneously playing the piano, my parents wisely arranged for me to take piano lessons. My teacher, a kind refugee from Hungary and a friend of my parents, offered to teach me for free. He had infinite patience, and I enjoyed the lessons while making quick progress. No one ever told me to practice. I remember dutifully practicing my violin for a few minutes every day and then rewarding myself by playing the piano! The contrast between my experience studying those two instruments could not have been greater. Learning to play the piano was one of my most pleasant childhood learning experiences.

After we moved to Switzerland, I finally quit playing the violin but continued taking piano lessons until my early twenties. I enjoyed playing classical music, and, much to my father's delight, we sometimes played duets. Our favorite was a Vivaldi sonata for violin and piano. My sister continued to play the violin as an adult, but sadly, my father never fulfilled his dream of a family quartet.

My teaching experiences

I have had a variety of teaching experiences with children and adults of all ages, which have helped shape my thinking about the learning process. As a teenager in Geneva, my first teaching experience was giving piano lessons to an eleven-year-old girl who lived in our apartment building. She was eager to learn, and I enjoyed teaching her for a few years and seeing her progress.

During the summer after I graduated from high school, I worked for a month as a demonstrator in a hands-on science exhibit for children at the Swiss National Exhibition in Lausanne. The interactive projects ranged from playing a logic game with a computer to assembling Egyptian pottery. I greatly enjoyed that teaching experience. The children eagerly explored the projects and equipment, asked questions, and never wanted to leave when their parents urged them to move on to another exhibit.

While studying at the University of Geneva, I offered private tutoring for a high-school student who struggled with algebra. However, he was not very motivated to understand it. I also worked occasionally as a substitute teacher for biology classes at the middle school level (ages 12 to 15). Unfortunately, I did not enjoy that experience. In one class, the students discovered ahead of time that there was going to be a substitute teacher (me), and half of them didn't even show up for the class! Normally, a class list with a seating chart would be on the teacher's desk, but they had stolen the class list. Therefore, I had no way of knowing which students were missing, so I could not report their absence. I did the best I could and taught the lesson to the students who chose to be there. That experience saddened me, and I wondered what had caused the children to have so little interest in school or in learning. It differed considerably from my previous experience with the eager children who explored the projects in the science lab.

Later, I spent a full year as a substitute teacher for a course on the history of science at the academic high school in Geneva (from which I had graduated only a few years earlier). I found that experience much more enjoyable than my previous substitute teaching experience at the middle school level. I had two separate classes, and I met with each class for only one hour each week. The highly motivated students were in their last year of high school, and all of them were planning to attend the university and pursue a career in science.

One of the homework assignments I gave my students was to research the life of a famous scientist of their choice (either living or dead) and write a short report about the person. Unfortunately, one student submitted a plagiarized report. I had seen the source that she had copied it from. Feeling shocked and confused, I could have referred her to the school administration, but that might have prevented her from graduating and attending the university. I decided to give her another chance, so I talked with her privately, told her that I knew her report was not her own work, and gave her a chance to rewrite it. With much embarrassment and gratitude for the second chance, she apologized for cheating and wrote another report.

At the University of California, where I earned a Ph.D. in psychology, I had a completely different kind of teaching experience. Curious about the learning process in both humans and animals, I participated in research with non-human primates (two chimpanzees and an orangutan) to assess their ability to learn basic number concepts. I found it fascinating to work with such intelligent animals and to figure out how best to teach them. I also conducted a study comparing two approaches to teaching three-year-old children a basic counting skill (the concept of one-to-one correspondence). There is more information about that study in Chapter 2.

After I earned my Ph.D., I taught introductory psychology at the university. I was responsible for teaching 30 first-year students the entire field of psychology in ten weeks (with four class meetings per week). I taught the same course five times over two years, with a different group of students each time. I was required to give a final exam and assign a grade to each student at the end of the course. However, I was free to decide which textbook to use, how to teach the course, and how to grade the students.

I decided to use a grading system that allowed every student to earn a good grade. I gave my students three chances to pass a weekly test, and I assigned four take-home projects involving a written report. If they completed all those assignments, they would automatically receive a passing grade. If they wanted to earn a higher grade, they had to pass the final exam. I enjoyed teaching those students, who were highly motivated to learn and succeed. I always asked them to complete anonymous evaluations at the end of the course, and I felt encouraged when several students described my class as the most enjoyable class they had ever taken!

As a mother, I taught my children a wide variety of skills and concepts, often at their request. For instance, they both wanted to learn how to play the piano, so I gave them lessons, first teaching them to play familiar songs by ear and then to read music. I recorded them when they began to compose their own simple tunes. Remembering that I had enjoyed playing the piano as a child without ever being told to practice, I never asked my children to practice or offered them any rewards. Sometimes, they would go months without touching the piano, but they always returned to it when they felt motivated to continue perfecting their skill. On some days, they would spend hours at the piano without any pressure from me. Both learned to play classical piano pieces by Bach, Mozart, and other composers without ever being told to practice.

For ten years, I gained teaching experience while volunteering at the alternative classroom that my children attended. On my weekly volunteer days, I created a math learning center in their classroom. I enjoyed setting up monthly hands-on math activities, including many homemade games. I loved working with the children, either individually or in small groups, to help them understand math concepts. I also contributed to the class by teaching songs and outdoor cooperative games, which the children loved.

One year, I worked with some of the children in the class to perform a play based on the book *Charlotte's Web* (by E.B. White). My son wanted to perform in this play because he liked the book, and he recruited volunteers from the class to participate (ages five to eight). The teacher agreed to let me supervise this project, and I let the children do most of the planning. They decided who would play each role, and they spent several weeks creating props, scenery, and costumes. During the performance on the stage in the school auditorium, I narrated the story while the children acted it out and spoke occasional lines, which they knew from the book. (In the next section, there is more information about that school.)

When my daughter was four years old, she enjoyed participating in my weekly outdoor classes for parents with their preschool-aged children. The class, called "Partners in exploration," involved meeting at a different location each week, such as a beach, a lake, a mountain trail, or a farm. We took walks and did science, craft, and music activities relating to each location. When she was between eight and twelve, I gained additional experience working with children by assisting the leader of her Girl Scout troop. I helped with projects, games, and camping trips.

More recently, I worked with adult learners by teaching an informal weekly French class for five years to four women. I loved finding ways to make the class fun. They enjoyed singing, so I taught them many French songs and used the lyrics to increase their vocabulary and illustrate grammatical rules.

Since 1984, I have been giving lectures, classes, and workshops about Aware Parenting for both parents and professionals in over twenty countries, as well as online. For several years, the first classes I offered were weekly meetings for mothers with their babies. I spent part of each meeting giving parenting information and support and the remainder of the time engaging the babies in playful activities. Each week, we focused on a specific type of stimulation, such as visual, auditory, or tactile. I also included singing, interactive play, and fun activities to stimulate the babies' memory and problem-solving skills.

When I compare and evaluate these various experiences, I realize that my most enjoyable teaching memories involve children or adults who were motivated to learn and whom I was not required to test or evaluate in any way. I love offering that kind of teaching.

My children's school experiences

When my son was four years old, I began to look for a school that would help him learn without damaging his self-esteem, curiosity, creativity, and motivation. I visited the local public school, just a few blocks from our home, to see what it was like. I observed a classroom for five-year-old children whose teacher was considered one of the best in the school district for children that age. Unfortunately, I was horrified by what I saw.

The day I visited the school, the children were learning how to write the capital letter M. The teacher gave each child a lined worksheet with blank rows, except for a large printed letter M at the beginning of each row. He instructed the children to complete each row with capital M's in a very specific way. He told them to use a different color for each of the four parts of the letter. First, they were to select a colored crayon and use it to write the first part of the letter. Then, they were to put that crayon back in the box and select a different color for the second part of the letter, and so on. A completed worksheet would contain several rows of capital M's, each consisting of four different colors. Apparently, his goal was to help the children learn that the letter M is composed of four lines.

Most of the children followed the teacher's instructions. After each child completed the worksheet correctly, the teacher placed a happy face sticker on it. However, one little girl chose to complete the worksheet differently. She picked up a red crayon and used it to complete *an entire row with the first part* of each letter M. Then, she picked up a green crayon and added the second part of each letter M in the entire row. She continued this approach with two other colors. This was obviously a much more efficient way to complete the task, and I loved seeing this evidence of innovative thinking. However, as she was happily and confidently finishing her worksheet, the teacher noticed her approach and told her that she was doing it wrong. He did not give her a happy face sticker, and she looked very disappointed.

It was extremely painful for me to witness such discouragement of a child's creativity and innovative thinking. I felt that the teacher's response damaged the child's confidence and self-esteem. I went home and cried, and I told my husband that we would *never* put our son in that school. I then visited some private schools in our city, including a Montessori school and a Waldorf (Steiner) school. I liked some of what I observed, but unfortunately, our financial resources at that time were not sufficient to pay for those schools. Before considering homeschooling, I tried one other option.

In California, where I live, there is a state law that allows public school districts to establish alternative educational programs if enough parents request them. I collaborated with other parents to request an alternative program in our local school district based on the educational philosophy of John Holt and other progressive educators. Our proposal was accepted, and both of my children attended that program for several years.

The children were free to follow their interests and learn at their own pace, and they had plenty of time for free play. They had no tests, no homework, and no grades. The program included many creative projects and field trips, and the teacher did not use punishments or rewards. Each year, the children participated in a book fair, a science fair, and a social studies fair, where they displayed their creative projects and experiments. Parent participation was mandatory; one parent from each family was required to participate in the classroom for a few hours every week or contribute their time in other ways, such as fundraising.

Without that program, my husband and I would likely have homeschooled our children, which was (and still is) legal in California. Thanks to the alternative program that I helped establish, my children's early school years were free of academic pressure, and they maintained their eagerness to learn. The following incident reassured me that the school was not damaging my son's motivation to study and learn.

On the last day of school before the summer holidays, when Nicky (my son) was eight years old, he brought home all his school belongings in a backpack. The next morning, while looking through his backpack, he noticed his math workbook, which he had not fully completed during the school year. He picked it up, grabbed a pencil, and sat at the dining room table, saying, "I never finished my math workbook. I'm going to do it now." He then spent an hour working on math problems. It was the first day of summer vacation, and that's what he chose to do!

At ten years of age, several of my son's friends had left the alternative program, and he no longer enjoyed the school as much as before. He also felt that he was not learning enough and asked if he could switch to a regular, traditional school. That indicated to me that he was ready for a more structured approach to learning, so, with trepidation, I transferred him to the closest public school. My daughter also decided to transfer to that same school a few years later (at the age of nine).

Both of my children adjusted well to the demands of traditional schooling. They were fortunate to have many compassionate, patient, and creative teachers, and they continued to do well in traditional public schools through high school and beyond. Although both experienced school stress and anxiety at times, neither of them lost their motivation to learn.

While writing this book, I interviewed Nicky (now in his forties) and asked him to share his memories of the alternative program. He mentioned the following benefits:

> I think it was beneficial in two ways. One is that it helped me delay the onset of school burnout. I had five years of play-based schooling (from ages five to ten), and I was not at all burnt out when I started regular school. Some of my friends were already burnt out by the age twelve or fourteen, and they didn't do nearly as well in high school as they could have. I was not burnt out yet, so I was able to benefit more from junior high school and high school. I was still eager to learn and more willing to do all the annoying and stressful aspects of school. Traditional schooling is about your tolerance for stress and busywork and doing things you don't want to do. I guess I was more willing to do that because I hadn't had to do it in the early years while other children my age were stuck sitting at desks and doing homework. Secondly, I gained social skills during those years in the alternative program because of all the free, undirected interactions with other children. I learned how to get along with all sorts of different kinds of people. I gained more social skills than I would have if

I had been in a much more rigid and structured school. Traditional schools are very artificial environments, and I don't think that children develop a full range of social skills in that setting. But I was able to do so in the alternative program, where we had lots of freedom.

Chapter 2

Learning by Discovery

> *"Learning is not the product of teaching. Learning is the*
> *product of the activity of learners."*
> —*John Holt*

THE YEARS I SPENT studying with Jean Piaget in Switzer-land further contributed to my understanding of children's natural learning processes. In this chapter, I begin with a brief overview of Piaget's theory of learning and contrast it with the behaviorist learning model. I describe two different approaches to teaching based on these two theories: learning through guided discovery and learning through direct instruction. In the final section, I discuss a topic related to discovery learning: the importance of concrete experiences in concept formation.

Piaget's theory of learning
Stages of cognitive development
As explained in Chapter 1, I took a two-year course taught by Jean Piaget while studying at the University of Geneva, Switzerland. I also participated in his advanced seminars and conducted a research study at his institute.

Piaget wrote many books about children's cognitive develop-ment. He theorized that children go through stages of development in their thinking and understanding of the world, specifically re-garding symbols, logic, mathematics, and moral concepts. His the-ory has important implications for education.

Piaget called the first stage of development the sensorimotor stage, which lasts from birth to about age two. During this stage, babies learn primarily through their senses and movements. They acquire some spatial concepts as well as basic ideas of cause and effect. During the second year, the ability for symbolic thought emerges, which is the understanding that certain things (such as words, numbers, or toys) can represent other things.

The second stage of development, called the preoperational stage, lasts from age two to age seven. This stage is characterized by spontaneous symbolic play and the rapid development of language, both of which indicate an ability to understand symbols.

Piaget also focused on what children *cannot* do at various ages. During the preoperational stage, he described children as "egocentric," but he didn't mean that they were selfish or that they lacked empathy. Instead, this term refers to their difficulty in seeing the world from other people's perspectives. To illustrate egocentrism, Piaget's used an example of two brothers. He asked one of the boys, aged five, if he had a brother, and the boy replied "Yes." Then he asked him whether his brother had a brother, and the boy replied, "No, there are just the two of us." Another example of egocentrism is that children of this age might not realize that they are blocking other people's views when they stand in front of them to watch TV.

Also, during the preoperational stage, children do not have a full understanding of numbers as abstract concepts, independent of the physical properties of objects. Instead, their immediate perceptions override their judgment of numerical quantities. For example, a three-year-old child typically thinks that the number of cookies changes when they are spread out over a wider space, but most seven-year-olds understand that the number of cookies does not change. For the same reason, a four-year-old child might prefer to receive five one-dollar bills instead of one five-dollar bill because the five bills appear to be more money.

The third stage of development, from age seven to age twelve, is called the concrete operational stage. This stage is characterized by the child's gradual ability to fully understand another person's perspective, as well as an understanding of numbers, basic mathematical operations, and principles of logic in real, concrete situations.

The final stage of development begins at about age twelve and is called the formal operational stage. At this stage, children's thinking no longer depends on real, concrete objects or situations. They can now apply logical reasoning to purely hypothetical situations, and they can fully understand the mathematical concept of probability as well as the scientific method of hypothesis testing.

How children learn

Piaget's basic theory is that children create organized patterns of thought, called "mental structures," as they interact with their environment and assimilate information. These serve as working models of how the world works, and they guide children's perception, thinking, and problem-solving. Children periodically revise and update these mental structures as they assimilate new information and experiences into their existing structures, discovering that the old ones are no longer accurate.

Each stage of development is characterized by a major revision in the child's basic mental structures. Piaget used the term "accommodation" to refer to this periodic revision. He compared children's cognitive development to the work of scientists, who periodically revise their theories to accommodate new research findings. Another way of explaining this is that, as children grow, there is not only a quantitative increase in their factual knowledge but also major qualitative changes in the way they think.

Piaget suggested three factors that help children progress from one stage to the next. First, he emphasized children's own movements and interactions with objects. For example, children gradually acquire abstract number concepts through repeated experiences of handling objects and moving them around.

The second factor that helps children progress from one stage to the next is the maturation of the brain. Interestingly, neuroimaging studies have shown brain changes in children that correspond to Piaget's stages of development. The third factor is social interaction with other people.

Piaget's work has important implications for education. The specific ages and stages can serve as a helpful guide for age-appropriate expectations of children. In addition, his theory about how children learn has inspired much research, leading to effective educational approaches, which are described in the next section.

Direct instruction versus learning by discovery

Piaget's concept of learning differs considerably from the behaviorist model of operant conditioning, which defines learning as the acquisition of specific behaviors, skills, or facts that have been reinforced by rewards. The behaviorist approach to learning also includes the reduction (or total disappearance) of behaviors through punishment. This behaviorist learning model, based on rewards and punishments, has been used throughout history to teach and discipline children. In the twentieth century, B. F. Skinner, an American psychologist, gave it scientific status through his research studies with rats and pigeons.

Piaget's theory of learning emphasizes understanding rather than the memorization of specific behaviors or skills, and he focused on how children acquire this understanding. He did not include direct instruction as one of the factors that enable children to progress from one stage to the next, and he never mentioned punishments or rewards. As explained in the previous section, he recognized children's contribution to the learning process in the form of internal working models, which resemble scientific theories. In Piaget's model, children are much more than empty vessels to be filled with knowledge.

Piaget's assumption was that children are born knowing how to learn by creating theories (mental structures), because their brains have been shaped by evolution to do so. Educators and researchers commonly use the term "constructivism" to refer to Piaget's theory that children construct knowledge and meaning from their experiences.

Young children's tendency to overgeneralize grammatical rules while learning to talk illustrates the differences between the behaviorist theory and the Piagetian constructivist theory. In English (and many other languages), most nouns are pluralized by adding an "s." For example, the plural for "book" is "books." However, for some English words (especially those of Germanic origin), plurals are not formed by adding an "s." For example, the plural of "foot" is "feet." Young English-speaking children typically learn the rule about adding an "s" before they learn these exceptions to the rule, and they overgeneralize the rule by forming incorrect plurals. They might say, for example, "My foots are dirty." These kinds of mistakes indicate that they have formed a theory about pluralization, and their theory results in utterances that they have never heard anybody say or that have never been reinforced in any way. The behaviorist model of learning has no simple explanation for this phenomenon, but it fits perfectly with Piaget's constructivist theory of cognitive development.

These two theories of learning (behaviorism and constructivism) lie at the root of two different approaches to teaching. Direct instruction is based on behaviorism, and the underlying assumption is that children are like empty vessels to be filled with knowledge. Teaching through guided discovery is based on constructivism, and it aligns with Piaget's theory that children construct knowledge out of their experiences.

Direct instruction implies teaching in the traditional sense of the word. Teachers give information, usually in verbal or written form. They might also show pictures or perform demonstrations. The children are expected to assimilate the information by listening and watching. They are told to study and memorize the information, and they are later tested and rewarded with good grades for correct answers.

The following example illustrates direct instruction in mathematics.

A math teacher in a class of 12-year-old children teaches the concept of pi by drawing a large circle on the blackboard and explaining that the distance around the circle is called the circumference. He then draws a line through the middle of the circle and explains that this line is the diameter. Next, he tells the class that the circumference divided by the diameter of a circle is a number called pi, which is 3.14. He explains that this number is the same for all circles, no matter how big they are. The children are told to memorize this number and are later asked to recall the definition and value of pi on a test.

In the guided discovery approach, teachers minimize direct instruction and think of themselves more as facilitators of learning. They provide children with objects, experiences, and problems to think about, and they help the children discover facts, concepts, or general principles. The guided discovery approach is more indirect, and the children are more actively involved. If tests are given, they are designed to assess the children's understanding of the material rather than their memory of specific facts.

The following example illustrates how I was taught the concept of pi by guided discovery during my last year at the progressive school that I attended in the United States.

When I was 12 years old, I had homework for the first time, and my math teacher gave an unusual assignment. I was told to find a round object at home, such as a bowl or a plate. Then I was supposed to measure the distance around it (the circumference) and the distance across the middle (the diameter). After that, the instructions were to divide the circumference by the diameter. I found a round waste basket at home and did the required measurements and division problem. The next day in class, our teacher asked each of us what kind of round object we had measured and what our measurements and answers were. He wrote all our measurements and answers in a column on the blackboard and then asked us what we noticed. We were surprised to see that all the answers were very close to the number 3. He asked us to think about why they were all so similar but not identical. Someone suggested that the number was probably bigger for larger objects, so we checked that theory, but it didn't match the data. Then someone suggested that the correct number would probably be 3 if we had more precise measuring instruments, but we noticed that all our answers were slightly above 3, and none were below, so we rejected that theory. Then we suggested that the answers would probably all be the same if we had more precise measuring instruments, but that the number was probably slightly more than 3. Our teacher confirmed our theory and told us that the circumference divided by the diameter would be identical for any circle and that it was called "pi." He also explained that the value of pi could be rounded to 3.14, but that it was actually a bit higher, because the decimals went on indefinitely. Later, we were given the following problem to solve: "What is the circumference of a circle with a diameter of ten centimeters?"

Children's brains are very good at learning by discovery, and their first accomplishments are always acquired through this method. We don't teach babies how to walk or form the past tense of verbs, and yet they learn to walk and talk without any instruction. By the time they go to school, they have acquired an amazing number of skills and a great deal of knowledge without any explicit teaching. Learning by discovery continues to be a natural and effective way for school-aged children, and even adults, to learn. However, some guidance can be helpful to facilitate discovery learning, hence the term "guided discovery."

The direct instruction approach is more effective for teaching facts (such as the names of the planets) and giving specific instructions (such as what to do in case of a fire). The guided discovery approach is more effective for helping children understand mathematics, science, and general concepts or principles in most other subjects.

Some subjects can be learned either way or with a combination of both approaches. Learning a foreign language in school usually involves direct instruction, with explanations of grammatical rules and the memorization of vocabulary words. However, children can also learn foreign languages through a discovery approach by exposing them to the language in real-life settings. Children who are immersed in a foreign language naturally figure out the meanings of words and grammatical rules without being taught. Some online software programs for learning foreign languages offer a direct instruction approach. Others emphasize learning by discovery by mimicking the method that children naturally use to learn their first language through immersion. The method offers learners opportunities to figure out grammatical rules and word meanings on their own.

When I was teaching psychology at the University of California, I conducted a research study comparing two approaches to teaching young children (ages two to three years) the concept of one-to-one correspondence, a basic math skill necessary for counting. One approach used direct instruction, and the other used a guided discovery approach inspired by Piaget's constructivist theory of how children learn. The results indicated that the children who learned through guided discovery had better long-term recall and performed better in situations that required them to transfer their understanding to new situations. These findings suggest that the guided discovery group acquired a deeper understanding of number concepts. My study was published in the *Journal of Educational Psychology*. (It is included in the references at the back of the book.)

Other researchers have found similar results: learning by discovery with a constructivist teaching approach is more effective across all ages than direct instruction. Studies indicate that constructivist teaching methods promote deeper understanding, better critical thinking skills, increased student interest and engagement, greater retention of material, and an improved ability to apply knowledge to real-world situations.

Memorizing specific facts is less important now than in the past, because information is easily accessible on the internet. At the same time, the importance of deeper understanding and logical thinking has increased. To accomplish this deeper kind of learning, we must engage children as active participants in the learning process and trust their natural ability to create meaningful learning out of their experiences.

The following chart summarizes the differences between these two approaches.

Comparison between direct instruction and guided discovery

Direct instruction	Guided discovery
Use of language and demonstrations to convey information.	Use of objects, experiences, or problems to think about.
Learners are passive recipients.	Learners are active participants.
Learners are encouraged to memorize facts.	Learners are encouraged to think.
Useful for specific information or instructions.	Useful for math, science, and general concepts or principles.
Learners cannot easily transfer knowledge to new situations.	Learners can transfer knowledge to new situations.
Limited long-term recall.	Stronger long-term recall.
Tests are used to assess memory of facts.	Tests are used to assess deeper understanding.

From concrete experiences to abstract thinking

Piaget's theory of learning also emphasizes that concept formation and abstract thinking arise naturally from concrete experiences.

Children need hands-on, concrete experiences with real objects and situations before they can understand abstract concepts represented by symbols. He emphasized the importance of physical movements during this learning process and even referred to children's mental theories as internalized actions.

As explained in the first part of this chapter, babies do not initially have the ability to understand symbols. However, they are busy gaining the concrete experiences that will help them understand symbols later. Language is a collection of abstract symbols representing real concepts and objects, and children must have concrete experiences with these concepts before words have meaning for them. For example, they must know what it feels like to touch hot and cold objects before the words "hot" and "cold" hold any meaning.

Babies also form basic logical concepts through their own experiences. For example, they acquire the concept of cause and effect when their actions cause something to happen. They learn that a rattle makes a noise when they shake it. This experience is crucial for understanding the abstract concept of cause and effect and the verbal expression "if...then."

After babies learn to crawl, they develop an understanding of spatial relationships by moving their body through space. They learn, for example, that they can crawl from the living room door directly to the couch, or they can take a detour by crawling first from the living room door to the window and then from the window to the couch. Through this process, they acquire the basic concept of a triangle, and they learn that crawling from point A to point B and then to point C achieves the same result as crawling directly from point A to point C. The concept of a triangle will be more meaningful if they have already had these types of experiences.

The same principle applies to number concepts. When young children sort and compare sets of objects, line them up according to size, or give one cookie to each family member, they are forming basic number concepts. When they build a stairway out of cubical blocks, they learn that each step must have one more block than the previous one. This experience forms the basis for their later understanding of the area of a triangle. Children need these concrete experiences with objects before they can fully understand mathematical concepts.

Hands-on experiences are an important aspect of learning by discovery because they help children develop an understanding of important concepts through their own actions. In the direct instruction approach, teachers often try to teach symbols and terms *before* the children have acquired the underlying concepts. However, symbols and terms can be taught more effectively, and will have deeper meaning for children, *after* they have already formed the underlying concepts through their own hands-on experiences.

_____

Chapter 3

Play and Stimulation

> *"Avoid compulsion, and let your children's*
> *lessons take the form of play."*
> —*Plato*

I OFTEN REFLECTED on my childhood while studying with
Piaget, and I realized that much of my understanding of the world
occurred outside of school, when I was engaged in play. In this
chapter, I share my childhood memories of play, using these examples to illustrate how learning can occur through play. I also offer
some examples and guidelines for providing appropriate stimulation by following children's interests.

My childhood memories of play
In Chapter 1, I described the school I attended until the age of
twelve, where I had no homework, tests, or grades until the last year.
This allowed me plenty of free time every day after school (which
ended at 3 PM) as well as on weekends and during the summer. I
enjoyed reading, but my favorite activity was playing, and I have
many fond memories of childhood play experiences. I never felt
bored and always found something to do.

We lived in a large house, and the entire attic had been con-
verted into a playroom. My siblings and I each had our own private
play area in addition to a shared central area. I remember setting up
a doll orchestra and a doll hospital in my play area. One year, my

mother helped us make puppets, and we performed puppet shows using a home-made puppet stage.

Our toys and activities were traditionally gender-typical, but that never bothered me. I loved playing with dolls, but I also enjoyed my brother's toys. One year, I helped him build a two-meter replica of the Eiffel Tower with his construction set. We even installed an elevator that actually worked. (I recommend offering a variety of toys to all children, regardless of their gender.)

I also spent much of my time outdoors in our backyard. One year, I spent several days creating a playground for my favorite doll, complete with a doll-sized swing, slide, wading pool, and sandbox. My siblings and I enjoyed playing badminton and throwing a basketball into a hoop attached to our garage.

I often rode my bicycle with my siblings and the neighborhood children. We enjoyed sidewalk games such as hopscotch, jacks, jump rope, and roller skating. On warm summer evenings, we all played hide-and-seek. In the autumn, we gathered piles of fallen leaves and jumped into them. In the winter, we built snow forts, had snowball fights, and pulled our sleds to a nearby hill. One of my favorite winter activities was ice skating on a frozen pond, and I loved creating stunts on ice (resulting in many hard falls).

Both of my parents loved board games, and we often had family game nights playing card games, Monopoly, or Scrabble. When I was six years old, my father taught me how to play chess. To make the game more balanced while I was learning, he gave himself a handicap by removing his queen (the most powerful chess piece). During long car rides, we played guessing games, such as hiding an imaginary object somewhere in the world or identifying roadside objects beginning with each letter of the alphabet.

One summer, my parents rented a cabin for a month on a lake in the remote wilderness of northern Minnesota. My grandparents rented the only other cabin on the lake. We had no other children to play with, but we had each other, books and games, the lake, the woods, and plenty of free time. That summer, my sister and I decided to write a book. For years before that, she had entertained me with stories of her own invention. She was only 16 months older than me, and we shared a bedroom. After our mother kissed us goodnight and turned off the light, my sister's stories would begin. One of our favorites was about two sisters who had a magic wishing tree that granted all their wishes. Every evening, she created a new adventure for the girls. During that summer at the lake, we decided to write the story down. I remember sitting by the lake with a notebook and pencil while my sister dictated. By the end of the month, we had filled an entire notebook with several chapters of a book called *The Wishing Tree*.

When I was ten years old, my mother showed me how to use her sewing machine, and I enjoyed designing and making clothes for my dolls. Our family created our own holiday cards every year. We children designed them and printed them ourselves using a carved linoleum template coated with ink (linoleum block printing).

I enjoyed collecting things. One summer, I collected fireflies and kept them in a jar overnight to observe them closely. During my first summer in the Swiss Alps at the age of twelve, I collected wild Alpine flowers, pressed them, identified them, and created a book of labeled wildflowers (which I still have). One day, I collected snails and stored them in a large open jar with leaves that I thought they would eat, only to discover the next morning that they had all escaped! I also had a stamp collection.

Another way my parents encouraged play and creativity was by choosing not to buy a television set. All my friends had TVs in their homes, but my parents believed that watching television was a waste of time. Sometimes, I felt left out of conversations that my friends had about TV shows (for example, the day my girlfriends excitedly discussed a popular singer called Elvis Presley, whom I had never heard of). However, as an adult, I am grateful that my parents didn't buy a TV. The absence of passive, screen-based entertainment in our home forced me to create my own entertainment through play and creative projects.

I realize that I had a privileged childhood. My parents could afford a large house with spacious front and back yards in a safe neighborhood. They also had the financial means to enroll me in a private, progressive school where there was no homework or pressure of any kind. They were available to spend time with me and provided me with enriching experiences such as museum visits, concerts, plays, and travel. They gave me books and toys and understood the importance of free play. They fully supported my creative activities by providing the materials I needed and allowing me the time, space, and freedom to pursue my interests. Finally, as a white child living in the United States, I did not experience racial discrimination.

I am aware that not all parents can offer their children these same experiences. However, please remember that you can create a stimulating learning environment for your children even if you live in a small apartment and have limited time or financial resources.

Three functions of play

In this section, I use examples mostly from my own childhood to illustrate several functions of play.

While playing, I developed coordination, balance, strength, and endurance. My active outdoor play included running, jumping, riding my bicycle, sledding, skating, playing badminton, shooting baskets, raking leaves, and shoveling snow. I did not engage in these activities to become physically fit; I did them because they were fun.

I also acquired social skills, including language skills, through daily interactions with my siblings and neighborhood children. We planned activities together, often engaging in heated debates and negotiations about rules and leadership while experimenting with both cooperation and competition. We all learned what it felt like to be excluded from a group, to be a leader that nobody followed, and to be part of a group with a dictator.

Many of the games and activities I enjoyed as a child contributed to my intellectual development. Playing card games and board games helped me develop math, logic, spatial, and memory skills. Scrabble and other word games enhanced by reading and spelling ability. Writing a book with my sister allowed me to practice writing. I used spatial skills to make doll clothes, build a doll playground, and construct an Eiffel Tower model. I also developed creative skills while designing holiday cards and doll clothes, making puppets, and putting on puppet shows.

Much of my childhood play also helped me to learn and assimilate new information. I learned about zoology and botany by collecting fireflies, snails, and flowers. My stamp collection helped me learn about different countries. Each stamp was like a tiny window giving me a glimpse into another culture. I developed an understanding of mechanical engineering concepts by helping my brother build a model of the Eiffel Tower. For instance, the elevator that we installed in the tower functioned with pulleys. My doll orchestra reinforced my understanding of how a real orchestra works. Making doll clothes helped me learn how clothing is made.

In addition to helping me learn new skills and assimilate information, play also helped me release stress and work through traumatic experiences. As an adult, I learned that symbolic play is especially effective in helping children work through traumatic experiences, and I instinctively engaged in this kind of play as a child. For instance, my doll hospital allowed me to process the emotions related to a traumatic hospital experience I had at the age of five. I tenderly cared for my dolls while pretending that they were sick in the hospital. When creating puppet shows with my own stories, I included arguments and other conflicts between the puppet characters, which helped me process feelings of jealousy toward my siblings. Using frightening puppets representing witches, ghosts, and monsters allowed me to confront my fears about evil and death while having complete control over the story's ending.

My childhood play was not only fun, it played a vital role in my education while also contributing to my emotional well-being. The following chart summarizes these benefits of play.

Three functions of play

- It helps children acquire physical, social, and intellectual skills.

- It helps children learn and assimilate new information.

- It helps children release stress and work through traumatic experiences.

Marion Rose shared the following example of her daughter learning a physical skill (swimming) through play and then practicing an intellectual skill while swimming:

> I remember, as if it were yesterday, when I first realized that children have an innate desire and ability to learn through play. My daughter was four years old, and we had just had a swimming pool built in our backyard. Over about three days, with our support and lots of fun, she simply learned to swim. During the following days, she made the shapes of letters and numbers with her body by swimming them, all for her own enjoyment.

Françoise Somers described how her daughter used play to assimilate information learned at school and also to release stress:

> My daughter has always enjoyed learning. When she first started going to school, she re-enacted her school day with dolls and stuffed animals as soon as she returned home. She taught them what she had learned that day and had them do homework. (That's how she developed a willingness to do her own homework at a young age.) This play allowed her to assimilate the information, and it was also

useful for releasing tensions from the day. The assimilation play was usually spontaneous and self-directed. However, the kind of play that allowed her to release school stress required more active participation on my part.

Rico Heinisch (a teacher in an alternative school in Germany) described how the children initiated a playful activity that resulted in meaningful learning:

> During our school's learning time, three children wanted to play "school" with me using stuffed animals. I used a stuffed animal to represent the teacher in a fictional classroom setting. At first, they couldn't think of what I should teach. Then, one child spontaneously decided to choose the moon as the subject. During the game, the children learned about the moon, the Earth, and the size ratio between the two. We used a globe and consulted books. An older child had initially decided not to participate, but when he overheard the other children misjudging the moon's size in relation to the Earth, he spontaneously joined in and shared his knowledge with the group.

In addition to illustrating playful learning, this example shows that children enjoy learning when they have a say in what and how they are taught. In the next section, I discuss the importance of following children's interests.

The importance of stimulation
Following children's interests
While raising my children, I noticed that active engagement and learning always occurred when I followed their interests. The following examples illustrate how I offered my children stimulation at different ages by paying attention to what they enjoyed doing:

At ten months old, Nicky (my son) dropped a rock into a wading pool and watched it sink. I gave him several more objects to drop into the pool, some of which sank and some of which did not. He enjoyed experimenting with them.

At three years old, Nicky picked up shells at the beach and wanted to take them home. I gave him a container to store his shells. When he spontaneously began grouping the shells based on their appearance, I provided him with several smaller containers for sorting them.

At eight years old, Nicky was fascinated by forts and castles, so I helped him find books about that topic at our local public library. One of the books described how to build a model of a Roman fort. When he expressed interest in building one, I provided him with the necessary materials.

At six years old, Sarah (my daughter) assigned a name and age to each of her dolls and stuffed animals. I gave her a sheet of paper and encouraged her to write them down. She was just beginning to read and write and loved the idea. She spontaneously created a chart with three columns: one for names, one for ages, and one for short descriptions.

At ten years old, Sarah became interested in codes after reading a detective story about a secret code. She found a book about codes at our local public library and created her own code book with each page featuring a different type of code. She had fun writing secret messages for others to decipher. I participated by decoding her messages and replying with coded messages of my own. She also enjoyed exploring the mathematical aspects of codes, such as letter frequencies and probabilities, and I helped her learn about those topics.

In these examples, there was always some form of initial stimulation: I provided my children with experiences, books, and toys.

I then built upon their interests by offering specific materials or guidance when they asked for it. I also ensured that they had plenty of time for unstructured free play and exploration.

Sometimes, the initial stimulation can spark a new interest and a lifetime of enjoyable learning, even leading to a career. My father-in-law received a paint set from his grandmother for his fourth birthday. That gift helped him discover that he enjoyed painting, and he grew up to become an artist.

When my husband bought an inexpensive, second-hand trumpet, he was aware that nobody in our family knew how to play it. When Nicky (age ten) saw it, he decided immediately that he wanted to play it. With the help of private lessons, he learned to play the trumpet and enjoyed performing in his school band and a youth orchestra throughout his teenage years. As an adult, he enjoys playing in a jazz band. I never told him to practice.

Encouraging children to think

Stimulation also includes encouraging children to think. My father often gave us simple math or logic problems to solve. One day at the dinner table, when I was nine years old, he asked us how many total handshakes there would be if each member shook hands with every other family member. There were five of us, and I felt very proud when I figured out the answer. He then asked us how many handshakes there would be with four or six people. In this way, he taught us to think and engage with mathematical concepts.

Remembering how much I had enjoyed my father's math problems at the dinner table, I gave my own children similar problems to solve during our family meals. Their love of my homemade cornbread provided a fun opportunity to introduce square numbers. I often baked cornbread in a square baking dish and sliced it into 16 evenly sized squares (four rows of four). My children preferred the four center pieces, which were moister and less crusty than the edge pieces. With 16 squares, there were four moist center pieces and twelve crusty edge pieces. I used this preference to ask them how many center pieces there would be if I sliced the cornbread into three rows of three or five rows of five. They enjoyed figuring it out, and this playful activity, which we called "cornbread math," helped them develop mathematical thinking in an enjoyable, real-life context.

The following example illustrates how I used a teachable moment to encourage my grandson to think when he visited us at nine years old:

> The plum tree in our backyard had become infested with aphids. We did not want to spray the tree with pesticides, so we bought a bag containing hundreds of live ladybugs, which are natural aphid predators. My grandson accompanied us to the store where we bought the ladybugs, and he watched as we released them under the plum tree. To our delight, the ladybugs soon spread throughout the branches. However, by the next morning, they had all disappeared, and the aphids were still there. My grandson found this puzzling and wondered what had happened to the ladybugs. I encouraged him to think of possible reasons for their departure, and together, we came up with more than ten theories to explain their disappearance. I also encouraged him to think of ways we could confirm or disprove our hypotheses. He loved this thinking exercise, which introduced him to the scientific method of observing, forming hypotheses, and testing them.

You don't need to own a big house or spend full time with your children to create a stimulating learning environment. Even if they attend a traditional public school, you can supplement their education by providing playful and engaging learning opportunities at home. By offering a few basic toys, books, and games, following their interests, answering their questions, providing materials for creative projects, and encouraging them to think, they will naturally integrate learning into their daily lives. There will be no need for coercion, bribes, or rewards.

Chapter 4

How Stress and Trauma Interfere with Learning

"A stressed child is not a learning child."
—Alice Miller

MY EXPERIENCE with schools as a student, a teacher, and a mother made me realize that specific aspects of schools can be highly stressful for children. I also witnessed how stress outside of school can affect children's ability to learn.

This chapter describes how stress and trauma affect the learning process. I begin by describing sources of stress outside the school environment followed by sources of stress within school. Despite the good intentions of parents and teachers, children can become stressed by teaching practices based on incorrect and outdated assumptions about how they learn. Some of these practices have effects that are not widely recognized. Several principles of learning are based on avoiding these harmful practices. In the final section, I describe the typical characteristics of stressed or traumatized children (post-traumatic reactions).

Stress and trauma outside the school environment
Sadly, many children do not feel safe in their homes or neighborhoods. Parental abuse, neglect, and substance abuse deeply affect children, as does living in unsafe, high-crime areas. Children whose

parents face financial difficulties, health or legal problems, bereavement, substance abuse, or divorce will inevitably be affected by this family stress.

Children who experience any kind of stress often struggle to concentrate and learn. Furthermore, they may lose interest in learning because they are too focused on basic survival. All children need to feel safe before they can learn, which is why creating safe learning environments in schools is so important. However, this alone may not be sufficient for children who live in threatening home or neighborhood environments.

Past traumatic experiences can also interfere with a child's ability to learn, even when their current lives are free of stress and threats. The effects of early abuse or neglect are well-documented and can continue to affect children's behavior, mood, and ability to learn long after the abuse or neglect has ended.

Some sources of trauma are not well recognized. Trauma can begin even before birth, and the birth process itself can be traumatic for babies, especially if medical interventions are needed to save their lives. Separation from the mother and placement in an incubator can also cause trauma. A mother's postpartum depression can feel like abandonment or separation-related trauma to a newborn baby and can interfere with bonding and attachment. Surgical procedures during infancy and early childhood can also deeply affect children, especially if they experience pain, physical restraint, or separation from their parents. These traumatic experiences are not the fault of the parents, so there is no need to feel guilty if they occurred in your family. However, it is important to be aware of their potential impact on your child.

Stressful aspects of schools

This section focuses on specific aspects of schooling and teaching approaches that can cause children to feel stressed, overwhelmed, anxious, confused, insecure, frustrated, or angry. I do not include the obvious kinds of school trauma that were common in the past, such as being hit or whipped for disruptive behavior or for making mistakes. Luckily, those abusive discipline practices are now forbidden in many countries. Instead, I focus on less obvious sources of stress that frequently occur in schools and are not often recognized.

My goal is not to criticize teachers, most of whom love children and genuinely want to help them learn. Many of these stressful aspects of schooling are not directly caused by teachers but by the nature of the institutions themselves, specifically the underlying assumptions on which teaching is based. Teachers are required to adapt to the educational system in which they work. They do not have much control over what or how they teach, how they assess their students' progress, or which disciplinary approaches they use.

In most schools, for example, teachers must give tests and grades and use an authoritarian approach to discipline that relies on rewards and punishments. They are also supervised and evaluated by the school principal, and their reputation (and sometimes even their salary) may depend on how well their students perform on tests. In addition, teachers may lack the training necessary to cope with children who struggle to learn or have behavior problems. When classes are large, teachers cannot meet all the students' needs, even though they may wish to give individual attention to specific children.

Separation from parents

For many children, especially very young ones, separation from their parents is a source of stress. In most countries, mandatory schooling begins between the ages of four and seven, but some children may not be ready to be separated from their family for a full day (or even half a day). Those children may feel frightened and overwhelmed as soon as their parents leave because they have no secure attachment figure to turn to for emotional support.

When my granddaughter was 17 years old, she shared the following memory of separation anxiety at school as a young child:

I had a lot of trouble whenever my parents would leave me. That always made me really sad. When they dropped me off at school, I would cry a lot. Sometimes our parents were allowed to visit us during lunch. One day, when I was in the first grade (age six), my dad came to sit with me during lunch, but I was upset when he left, and I cried a lot in class afterward. My teacher came over to me and said that I shouldn't be crying, and that if I was going to cry, then my parents shouldn't be allowed to visit. It made me very upset, and I was also confused about why I wasn't allowed to cry in school. My parents were always okay with me crying at home, so I didn't know why my teacher was so upset about it.

Joss Goulden described the trauma of separation when she was sent to a boarding school at eight years of age:

I experienced significant school trauma when I was sent away to boarding school at the age of eight. I felt unsafe, alone, unsupported, and in danger much of the time. I experienced daily shame and punishment, without guidance or support to navigate the stress. I was forced to dissociate from the pain and be in a state of chronic nervous system trauma response. Feeling abandoned by my parents was deeply painful. I missed my family, pets, and friends, and I experienced a devastating yearning to be back home. Being captive at school with no freedom, no choice, no agency, and no reprieve was extremely hard. I chose to homeschool my children for many reasons, but one of them was the understanding that being separated from your parents at a young age for five days a week is often traumatic for children.

Unfamiliar rules and expectations

Some children feel stressed by unfamiliar rules and expectations regarding their behavior. For example, children who are free to talk at home whenever they wish might feel confused and frustrated by a school requirement to raise their hands before speaking and to wait for the teacher's permission to do so.

Many children find it difficult to sit still for long periods of time without the freedom to stand, move, play, or even lie down as much as their bodies require. Most schools allow periods of play and movement, but this might not be sufficient for all children. Those who find it difficult to sit still might fidget in their seats, fall to the floor, pass notes to their friends, or throw things when they think the teacher isn't looking. These behaviors often stem from a simple need for more movement.

In some schools, children are free to use the bathroom whenever they want, but in others, they must wait for scheduled breaks between classes. Additionally, they might not be allowed to eat when they are hungry. Such rules, restrictions, and expectations can cause stress and may encourage children to ignore their physical needs for movement, food, and bathroom use, which is not healthy for growing bodies.

The classroom seating arrangement can seem unfamiliar and disorienting to children accustomed to family gatherings where people sit around a dinner table or in a living room. Such circular seating differs significantly from the traditional classroom setup, in which the children sit in rows of desks facing a teacher at the front of the room. This arrangement can leave children feeling isolated and disconnected because of their inability to see the faces of the other children.

Many children are used to playing and engaging in self-initiated projects at home or in a play-based preschool before they reach school age. After they begin school, they may find it confusing, difficult, or meaningless to learn isolated facts and skills through teacher-imposed methods that do not align with their natural ways of learning.

Christoph Geiger described his son's experience in a traditional school in Germany:

> My son (age six) has been in school since September. The teacher expects a high pace of learning and gives a lot of homework. After six weeks, during his fall break, he started his own projects. He created a book with a picture on each page and some written information about each picture. For example, on a page with a picture of a turtle, he wanted to write about turtles: what they eat and where they live. With our support, he was able to complete his book with the written information. When the holidays were over and it was time to go back to school, he said, "I don't want to go to school." What bothered him the most was sitting for long periods of time and not being allowed to spend much time outside. How nice it would be if the school allowed him to do the kind of projects that he spontaneously did at home.

Children can also experience stress and confusion when teaching methods differ from their cultural background. In countries affected by colonization, children from indigenous cultures might feel confused and disoriented by the school system's unfamiliar approach to teaching, which often reflects the dominant culture's assumptions about learning.

Indigenous ways of learning often differ greatly from those used in schools established by colonizing nations. In many indigenous cultures, children acquire skills and knowledge by observing the natural world and imitating and helping adults work in a spirit of mutual collaboration. Rather than receiving constant direct instruction, children are given specific guidance only as needed. Additionally, storytelling (often conducted in a circular seating arrangement) is a primary method of passing down knowledge.

Children from indigenous cultures might feel confused when they are required to memorize isolated facts without any meaningful context or when they are not permitted to collaborate with their peers. The concepts of individual achievement and competition may seem strange to them, and they might wonder why the school fails to acknowledge or value their culture's approach to learning.

Sexist or racist stereotyping and discrimination

In many countries, racial minorities, refugees, and immigrants experience discrimination and injustice in schools. In the United States, for example, research suggests that black children are systematically punished more often and more harshly than white children for the same behavior. Even kind and loving teachers can be influenced by the dominant culture in which they live and can have unconscious biases, assuming that certain groups of children are less intelligent or require stricter discipline. Unfortunately, such attitudes can make children feel bad, stupid, or even unsafe, and can prevent them from reaching their full potential.

Children can also suffer from gender-based discrimination in school. For example, when my daughter was eleven years old, she came home from school one day and said, "I hate my math teacher!" I asked her why, and she explained that the teacher treated the boys differently from the girls. Whenever the children raised their hands to answer questions, the teacher called on the boys more often, even though girls, including my daughter, had also raised their hands. This unequal treatment made her feel that the teacher did not expect girls to excel at math and that the subject was more important for boys. I told her that her anger was entirely justified.

Tests and grades

Tests and grades can be major sources of stress and anxiety for children. As an adult, my son shared the following memory from his childhood:

I was in a progressive alternative school until the age of ten. When I transferred to a regular school, I have a very distinctive memory of the first time I failed a test. We were supposed to memorize the names of the U.S. states and label them on a map. I don't think that I had ever had a test like that before: something that I was supposed to study for and memorize on my own. I remember feeling bad about myself for getting a failing grade. I wasn't expecting to be graded on that test. I remember feeling shocked and very frustrated with myself for not studying. I definitely blamed myself and not the school. It didn't occur to me that the teaching method was problematic. Instead, the lesson I learned from that experience was that I needed to "play the game," which meant study and memorize what I was supposed to learn. For a long time after that, in high school, and even in college, I became an over-studier, making sure that I really knew the material, because there was always a risk of failure. I definitely had anxiety. I don't think that grades are useful.

The possibility of failure is inherently stressful for children, which is why tests can cause considerable anxiety. In my son's case, this anxiety caused him to study more than necessary. However, for some children, it can interfere with their ability to concentrate.

Unfortunately, assigning letter or numerical grades based on tests and homework is a common but harmful practice in traditional public schools. In the United States, teachers typically assign letter grades from A through D, with F indicating failure. In the Swiss schools that I attended, grades were numerical, with six being the highest.

Online quizzes that provide immediate feedback can be a helpful study aide for children over eight years old. By that age, many children naturally enjoy striving for mastery and might enjoy the challenge of attaining 100% correct answers on an online quiz. However, even digital feedback can be stressful, especially when mistakes are corrected with a human voice saying "wrong!"

Because of the stress associated with the use of tests and grades, it is worth considering alternative ways to evaluate children's learning. Fortunately, tests are not the only way to accomplish this. Children welcome opportunities to demonstrate what they have learned by showing writing samples, drawings, or projects, especially when they know that they will not be graded on their work. Teachers usually have a fairly accurate idea of each child's progress, and they know which ones need extra help. A portfolio of a child's work or a teacher's written assessment can convey more meaningful information to parents than a grade based on test scores.

Humiliation and punishment

All forms of humiliation and punishment are harmful, and they have no place in parenting or education. Although corporal punishment has been banned in public schools in many countries, it has often been replaced by other forms of punishment, which can interfere with children's ability and motivation to learn.

Joss Goulden described her experience with shame and humiliation at her boarding school:

> If I did "badly" in an exam, I was shamed, humiliated, and punished. I remember feeling nauseous at exam time, unable to sleep, and very uncomfortable in my body. There was no awareness from teachers or parents that these experiences were challenging for me or that my accumulated stress and trauma might be affecting my ability to learn or perform in tests.

Even in the absence of humiliation or punishment, receiving a bad grade can feel like punishment to a child and may cause discouragement, low self-esteem, and reduced motivation to learn.

Good grades, praise, and rewards

It's easy to understand why giving children a low grade can cause stress, damage their self-esteem, and make them feel stupid. However, it's more difficult to understand how good grades, praise, and rewards can also contribute to children's feelings of insecurity.

We naturally want to encourage children to learn and to feel good about themselves. With that goal in mind, many people assume that children benefit from praise. But is this assumption correct? Many people praise children with words such as, "Good job," "Good girl," "You're really smart," "That's a good drawing," or "That's an excellent answer!" Unfortunately, this kind of praise may not be the best way to motivate children, help them learn, or boost their self-esteem.

Using praise that includes value judgments can have the opposite effect of what we want and can lead to anxiety, insecurity, and low self-esteem. This idea may seem surprising at first, but it's quite logical. If we tell a child, "You're really smart," when she correctly solves a math problem, she may feel stupid the next time she makes a mistake. In fact, she may become anxious or insecure while doing math for fear of failing to meet our expectations regarding her intelligence.

Children are born with the desire and the ability to learn, and they naturally take pride in their progress. They don't care whether their accomplishments are "good" until we start praising or rewarding them.

Joss Goulden recalled how praise caused stress for her:

> There were times at school when I performed highly, particularly in music and some sports. I was then praised and had the momentary experience of feeling a sense of worthiness and love. However, this was also distressing because it made me dependent on external validation, and when I performed badly, it was even more painful.

Another problem with praise, good grades, and other kinds of rewards is that children may begin to depend on external approval and lose touch with their inherent desire to learn. This negative aspect of rewards is discussed in Chapter 8.

Competition

Competitive learning environments can create stress for children. Contests such as "Let's see who can get the most answers right" or "Let's see who can finish first" may seem like a fun way to motivate children. Unfortunately, such practices can cause anxiety and damage friendships. Children who lose contests often feel inferior and resentful. Some give up trying, convinced that they will never be able to outcompete other children. Others resort to cheating.

Cooperative learning environments, on the other hand, can increase motivation and enhance learning, while avoiding the stress associated with competition. Instead of encouraging children to compete against each other, teachers can suggest group goals that allow all the children to succeed together, while encouraging mutual collaboration. Working on problems or projects in small groups can be an effective way to help children learn. During group work, children practice communication skills, share ideas, and learn from each other.

Forced learning

As illustrated in previous chapters, children learn eagerly when the topic arises from their own curiosity and interests. Conversely, when children are forced to learn or study something that does not interest them, the experience can be stressful, and they might not learn much.

It is difficult to cater to each child's interests in schools because teachers must usually follow a set curriculum. However, any approach that allows choices and self-direction is beneficial. Even small choices can be helpful while working within the curriculum. Additionally, children can help decide *how* they want to be taught.

Failure to understand something

Painful feelings of stress, anxiety, and incompetence can arise when a child fails to understand the topic being taught, the instructions, or test questions. These situations can be painful for children, especially when they observe other children who apparently understand better than they do.

Here is a painful memory from my childhood:

> One day, when I was seven years old, I failed to understand the teacher's instructions in class. She explained what we were supposed to do and then gave each of us a sheet of paper. I didn't understand the assignment and began to cry. An assistant teacher took me out of the room and asked me kindly why I was crying. As I tried to suppress my tears, I got the hiccups and found it difficult to talk. Furthermore, I felt too embarrassed to tell her that I hadn't understood the instructions, especially since all the other children had apparently understood. I felt greatly relieved when she excused me from the assignment due to my hiccups!

Immigrant children can experience daily stress as they struggle to understand an unfamiliar language. I experienced that kind of stress when I started attending schools taught in French after we moved to Europe. I often failed to understand what the teacher said, and I remember feeling mentally exhausted at the end of each school day from the constant effort to understand the language.

Children with dyslexia experience frustration and mental exhaustion not only while learning to read but also long after they have learned because of the extra effort required for them to process written material.

Failure to understand something can also result from a mismatch between the teaching approach and the child's preferred learning style. Children have different strengths and preferred ways of learning. For example, children with strong visual/spatial skills might understand illustrations better than verbal instructions. Similarly, children who learn best through movement might grasp mathematical concepts better through movement and rhythm than through written exercises.

Criticisms and corrections

Being criticized or corrected can often cause stress for children. At age 17, my granddaughter shared the following memory from first grade (when she was six years old):

> I remember one day when we were doing an art project, making little animals out of clay, and we were supposed to do it a certain way. I was doing it wrong, so my teacher thought I wasn't listening. I started crying when she criticized me harshly, and then she got mad at me for crying and sent me to the principal's office. That teacher seemed to have a hard time whenever I cried in class, and I think she wanted to get rid of me for crying. And she also told me that I wasn't allowed to finish the project. I don't know why.

Criticism can also be nonverbal. My granddaughter recalled another memory from that same year:

> I volunteered to read a book that I really liked in front of the class. But I was struggling with it so much that the teacher pulled it away from me and didn't let me finish it. I was very sad.

After other similar incidents, my son removed his daughter from that school.

It's easy to understand why criticism might discourage children and lower their confidence and self-esteem. But what about corrections offered lovingly, without any overt criticism? Most teachers assume that their job is to correct children's mistakes, and in many learning situations, corrections can be useful and even necessary. However, corrections can also make children feel discouraged, anxious, or incompetent, even when we don't humiliate, criticize, punish, or grade them. Therefore, it's important to be aware of how and when we correct children's mistakes and to do so in a respectful way.

In a method called "invented spelling" (also known as "developmental spelling"), teachers encourage children to write stories without correcting their mistakes. Children are more likely to enjoy writing, develop self-confidence, and be creative, when they don't need to worry constantly about spelling the words correctly. Most children naturally correct their own spelling errors as they gain more experience with written words, just as they learn to speak their native language correctly. Some may require more help, but they quickly lose interest in learning to spell with an approach based on a teacher's corrections of worksheets, homework, and tests. Instead, spelling instruction can be integrated, as needed, into enjoyable activities involving reading and writing. (Note that in some languages, such as French, correct spelling requires an understanding of grammar.)

When children are involved in meaningful projects, they often welcome information and corrections that help them reach their goals. I noticed that kind of motivation when I worked with some of the children in my son's class to perform a play based on the book, *Charlotte's Web* (mentioned in Chapter 1). The children wanted to create written signs to use as props for their performance because the words played an important role in the story. Highly motivated to spell the words right, they asked me to correct their spelling.

Being rushed and timed

Most schools aim to fit all children into the same timetable because it is the easiest way to manage a classroom. When teachers ask children to complete an assignment at their desks, the teachers naturally find it convenient to allocate the same amount of time for everyone. Unfortunately, some work more slowly and don't have time to finish, while others complete their work quickly and finish early. Those who don't have time to finish an assignment in class are often expected to complete it as homework (or stay after school to do so). Those who finish early often become bored. Both situations can be stressful for children.

Another disadvantage of rushing slower children is that they may try to work faster, but at the cost of neatness, thoroughness, accuracy, or deep thinking. Creative teachers find ways to avoid these problems by allowing sufficient time for the slower children and by finding interesting activities for the quicker ones to do while waiting for the slower ones to finish.

Timed tests are even more stressful. When children are evaluated and graded on the number of questions they complete within a limited time, those who are slow, conscientious, neat, and thorough are at a huge disadvantage. They often feel anxious and frustrated during the test and become upset if they receive a low grade. Children should never be tested for speed in learning situations. All children should be allowed as much time as needed to answer all the questions.

Mistreatment by other children

Many children suffer from bullying, exclusion, teasing, threats, and physical assault at school because of their behavior or appearance (such as height, weight, skin color, hair style, disability, or clothing). Children are also often bullied and shunned when their behavior does not conform to gender stereotypes. For example, boys who are highly sensitive or avoid rough sports are often teased and accused of being gay. If your child is experiencing teasing, exclusion, or bullying at school for any reason, it's important to inform their teacher and the school principal. Children cannot learn effectively if they do not feel safe or accepted for who they are.

Homework

A final source of school-related stress is homework. There is no evidence that homework has any educational value for children under the age of ten to twelve. Unfortunately, many schools give homework to children as young as five or six, and this can be a source of stress for both them and their parents. Some schools give so much homework that the children have little time to relax and play after school or on weekends. Slower children suffer even more from this lack of playtime, as they require more time to complete assignments.

My son shared his thoughts about homework from his point of view as a parent:

> I believe that homework for children damages the parent–child relationship. When my children were in elementary school (up to age eleven), they weren't developmentally ready to remember to do homework and weren't interested in doing it. This meant that we parents were expected to be the enforcers of this homework. I found myself torn between not wanting to do this but having to convince my children to do their homework, which is something that neither of us wanted to be doing. There were many other things we could have been doing that were far more educational than the homework assignment and also much more pleasant.

In the next chapter, I offer suggestions for helping children cope with various sources of school stress, including homework.

Stressful aspects of schools

- Separation from parents
- Unfamiliar rules and expectations
- Sexist or racist stereotyping and discrimination
- Tests and grades
- Humiliation and punishment
- Good grades, praise, and rewards
- Competition
- Forced learning
- Failure to understand something
- Criticisms and corrections
- Being rushed and timed
- Mistreatment by other children
- Homework

Characteristics of stressed and traumatized children

When children experience a traumatic event or an accumulation of stress at home or at school, their nervous system interprets that experience as a threat to their well-being and even survival. It automatically switches to survival mode, which involves one of two primary reactions: hyperarousal or dissociation.

Hyperarousal, also known as the fight-or-flight response, is a physiological state that allows children to confront an imminent threat by either defending themselves (fight) or escaping from the situation (flight). This means that their entire body is prepared for action. Common behaviors associated with hyperarousal include agitation, hyperactivity, impulsivity, and aggression. Children in this state may be disruptive and destructive. They often struggle to sit still for long periods and have difficulty concentrating.

Dissociation is a protective response designed to enhance survival by conserving energy in situations where fight or flight would not be possible or effective. Children in a state of dissociation feel threatened but don't show it. Instead, they appear calm, but this calmness is actually a numb and dreamy state, which is different from true relaxation. They are unresponsive and don't show their emotions. Like hyperaroused children, those who dissociate also have trouble concentrating.

These two reactions to stress and trauma correspond to distinct physiological states. Children who suffer from unhealed traumatic experiences and who are *also* experiencing current stress in their lives often find it very difficult to concentrate and learn. It is obvious why these posttraumatic states are not conducive to learning. From an evolutionary perspective, when a child's brain and body are primarily concerned with immediate survival, learning new information does not have a high priority.

When traumatized children lack opportunities to recover emotionally, any situation that resembles their original trauma can trigger these same reactions of hyperarousal or dissociation. For some children, these states become chronic, especially if they never feel totally safe. Children with these behaviors are often given a psychiatric diagnosis.

In addition to these outward manifestations of stress and trauma, these children also experience painful emotions such as anxiety, sadness, powerlessness, frustration, and anger. They may suffer from nightmares, sleep disturbances, and separation anxiety.

Fortunately, children can recover from stress and trauma. The next chapter explains how you can help your children cope with stress, heal from trauma, and regain their ability to concentrate and learn.

Chapter 5

Emotional Support to Help Children Learn

"The most important factor in child development is not what parents do, but who they are to the child—a source of safety, connection, and unconditional love."
—*Gabor Maté*

IN THE PREVIOUS chapter, I described some of the major sources of stress both in and out of school. Unfortunately, you cannot prevent all stress in your children's lives. However, you can offer emotional support to help them cope with stress and recover from trauma.

In this chapter, I explain how you can increase children's motivation, concentration, and thinking ability by helping them recover from stressful or traumatic experiences. I also offer tips for supporting children with homework assignments and for providing feedback without relying on praise, criticism, or corrections. The chapter concludes with a section on coping with your own feelings.

Helping children recover from stress or trauma

Fortunately, children are born with the ability to recover from stressful or traumatic experiences. We can reverse the effects of stress and trauma by supporting children to use their natural healing processes, which include crying, play, and laughter. For more information about these healing mechanisms, please see my book, *Healing Your Traumatized Child.*

Creating physical and emotional safety

The first step in helping your children recover from stressful experiences at school is to create emotional safety for them at home. This means ensuring that their home environment does not replicate the same types of stressful situations that they encounter at school. It also means being willing to listen to them talk and complain, while accepting their feelings without blaming, judging, or offering unsolicited advice. If they tell you that they failed a test, they don't need criticism or blame. For example, it is not helpful to say, "Maybe you didn't study enough." Instead, a more supportive response would be, "How do you feel about that?"

It's also important to let your children know that you are always on their side and that you support them. You may feel tempted to explain the teacher's point of view and justify the teacher's behavior, but doing so will not help your child feel supported. If your child returns from school saying, "My teacher is mean. She took my test away before I had finished," you might feel inclined to reply that the teacher has a schedule to follow and cannot allow a test to last all day. While this may be true, such a comment does not offer the emotional support your child needs. Instead, you can say, "I'm sorry to hear about that. It must have been very frustrating for you."

When you provide this kind of support, your children will feel safe enough to share their deeper emotions with you, which is an essential step in recovering from school-related stress.

Accepting children's tears

While raising my children, I noticed that they often cried because of school-related stress. Crying is an important healing mechanism, and children benefit when they are allowed to cry freely. If you have created a home environment in which your children feel safe to express their emotions, they will probably cry when they need to.

The following example illustrates how I supported my daughter's crying about a disagreeable homework assignment:

At the age of ten (after Sarah had transferred to a traditional public school), she was given a homework assignment to research an ocean animal and write a short report. Rather than allowing the children to choose their own animals, the teacher told each child which one to write about. Sarah would have loved to write about dolphins, so she was deeply disappointed when she learned that her assigned animal was tuna fish. After school that day, she had an angry crying fit at home about the tuna fish assignment. With tears streaming down her face, she yelled, "I don't even LIKE tuna fish!" I calmly listened to her outburst while acknowledging her feelings. I wanted her to feel safe to express her emotions, so I did not try to reason with her or calm her down. After twenty minutes of hard crying, with my support and attention, she calmed down on her own and reluctantly accepted that she would have to write a report about tuna fish. The next day, she found a book about tuna fish in the school library, and I helped her figure out what to include in her report.

This example illustrates the stress that can arise when children are forced to study a topic they are not interested in. My daughter wrote a lovely report and even received a good grade, but she did not enjoy the experience, and I don't think she learned much from it.

Françoise Somers described her daughter's need to cry before she was able to complete her math homework:

One day, when my daughter was seven years old, she had a homework assignment with math problems. Very quickly, she started to get angry and cry. She said that she did not understand the instructions and that she was being asked to do something impossible. I supported her and stayed with her in her anger while acknowledging that she was having a really hard time. I don't remember how long it lasted, but after she cried as much as necessary, she spontaneously returned to the table and did all the math problems without any apparent difficulty. She clearly understood the material and was able to do all the exercises without any mistakes.

The need to cry over school-related stress continues into adolescence. The following personal experience occurred during my last year of high school in Geneva, Switzerland:

As final exams approached, my classmates and I felt extremely stressed because our entire future depended on passing them. A few weeks before the exams, an incident occurred in our history class. The teacher made a critical remark to a girl who was physically disabled and used a wheelchair, and she burst into tears. Almost immediately, about half the students in the class also started crying, and one student even yelled at the teacher! Such behavior was unheard of in our school, where we were expected to show respect toward our teachers. (I felt like crying too, but I wasn't comfortable doing so in front of my classmates.) The teacher apologized to the girl he had criticized, but he clearly had no idea how to handle an entire classroom of distressed teenagers!

When crying is triggered by a minor incident, as in this example, I use the term *broken cookie phenomenon*. The teacher's critical remark provided a pretext for crying, but the *real reason* was the overwhelming anxiety that we all felt about the upcoming exams. We probably all needed to have a good cry, and almost anything would have triggered our tears.

If the teacher had understood the true cause of our emotional outburst and the healing effect of crying, he might have felt more comfortable with the situation. Teachers are not trained as therapists, and nobody expects them to do psychotherapy in the classroom. However, when children experience strong, painful emotions at school, a basic understanding of the benefits of crying can be helpful.

This information is also helpful for parents. If your child bursts into tears over a minor incident at home (such as a broken cookie) after a stressful day at school, the crying might have nothing to do with the incident. It's more likely that the underlying cause is the child's accumulated stress, and the minor event simply serves as a pretext to start crying. This broken cookie phenomenon can be difficult to understand because the intensity of the crying appears to be out of proportion to the triggering event.

When teachers understand the healing effects of crying, they can intervene in helpful ways to cope with children's aggressive behavior. Rico Heinisch described a supportive intervention he did with two angry boys at his school:

> In our school, we had two boys, aged nine and eleven, who had both been victims of violence at another school. One day, following an argument in which they both saw themselves as victims, they got into a physical altercation, pulling on a sweater. I stepped between them. The younger boy stood behind me while the older boy repeatedly tried to get to him. I calmly reminded the older boy of our school rules: we do not hurt others, we do not hurt ourselves, and we do not break things. I made sure to move slowly with open hands and arms, staying calm, but also reacting quickly when he attempted to attack the other boy again. I empathized with him, reflecting his feelings, telling him that I could see how desperate and angry he was. He began to share how unfair he felt things were, how no one ever acknowledged what he had been through, and how upset he was that his expensive sweater was ruined. When he began to scream and cry intensely about his experiences of injustice, I knew we were on the right track. He was able to

rage and cry, expressing many of the traumatic experiences from his previous school. It was positive for our teaching team to see that none of the younger children in the next room became frightened. We could see that the children in our school were okay with big feelings being felt and expressed.

Supporting children through play

In chapter 3, I mentioned that play can help children release stress and recover from traumatic experiences. A basic form of therapeutic play is one in which an adult simply pays attention to the child during free play in a room with a variety of toys. The adult does not direct the play or make any suggestions. The official name for this kind of play is "nondirective, child-centered play." It can be highly effective in helping children recover from traumatic experiences.

At six years of age, my granddaughter had some traumatic school experiences (described in Chapter 4). In the following example, I explain how I used nondirective, child-centered play to help her recover:

> When my six-year-old granddaughter attended a traditional public school, she experienced various kinds of school stress, which interfered with her enjoyment of school and her confidence in learning. One day, I spent an hour giving her my full attention while she played with her dolls. She spontaneously created school scenes involving interactions between children and teachers. I let her direct the play, but she welcomed my participation. Together, we enacted scenes that became increasingly silly, featuring children getting in trouble for doing things that they weren't supposed to do. She laughed a lot during this activity. When she was 17 years old, I asked her if she remembered that day when we had played the school game with her dolls, and she recalled it vividly.

Corinne Sprecher described how she helped her son recover from painful experiences in a Judo class by engaging him in a playful activity:

> When our son, Paul, was five years old, he participated in weekly Judo classes for young children and enjoyed them very much. After one year, he moved to a class with older children. The first session in that new group was not a pleasant experience for him. It started off in a painful way, when the teacher told the group, "I bet everyone will be faster than Paul." His intention was to play a game, and he did not expect Paul to be the slowest, but Paul was indeed the slowest. This was not at all a supportive experience for starting off in a new group with other children, some of whom were four to five years older than he was. Paul did not want to return to the Judo class, and we agreed that he could join the group of younger children again. Several months later, after he had earned his half-yellow belt, he wanted to try the class with older children again. Unfortunately, something unpleasant happened again. Before the class started, Paul got stuck in the bathroom stall and could not unlock the door until someone rescued him. After that, he did not feel ready to participate in the class, so he sat and watched. We decided not to switch him back to the group of younger children again but to support him with the transition. We told him that he could take as much time as he needed and that he could watch the class instead of participating. In addition, I initiated a game at home where I said, "I bet I am the fastest!" and then ran to the other side of the room. I always let Paul win. He loved the game, and we played it every day. Through this game, we helped him recover from the painful experience he had the first time he had joined that class. After only a week of playing it, Paul willingly participated in the new class. Now, he enjoys Judo a lot and feels competent and

confident. Since then, he has also successfully passed two more belt exams.

In this example, the child experienced two traumatic events in the class with older children: losing a race and being trapped in the bathroom. The bathroom incident might not have discouraged him from participating in the class if he hadn't had the earlier traumatic experience. However, it probably triggered his feelings of power-lessness and incompetence resulting from the earlier incident. The playful activity that Corinne initiated with her son is called "pow-er-reversal play" in Aware Parenting. The adult pretends to be weak or incompetent so the child can win. Power-reversal play is highly effective in helping children overcome feelings of powerlessness resulting from traumatic experiences.

It is important to trust children and allow them to make as many choices as possible while learning to do new things. However, when fears caused by traumatic experiences prevent them from doing what they truly want, therapeutic interventions can help. In Paul's case, he wanted to be in the more advanced class, which matched his skill level. Instead of giving in to his fears, his mother helped him overcome them through therapeutic play.

Stress can also result from painful social interactions at school. Many children experience teasing, bullying, or exclusion from peers. Joss Goulden described how she supported her son through both crying and play to help him recover from a challenging day at school:

My son attended school for just one year at the age of four. It was a small community school near our home. He did not want to be left alone, so I chose to stay with him for the two days a week that he was there. Despite my presence, he experienced some very scary harshness one day from an older child who teased, criticized, and threatened him. That evening at home, I noticed that he had some accumulated feelings, which was often the case after a long day at school.

I moved in with some connection and then invited him to share. He recounted the experience while I listened with compassion, and he had a big emotional release with crying, raging, and active body movements. After he stopped crying, I talked with him about what had happened, and we joked about all the things he might want to do or say to that child. In the next few days, I offered him additional play opportunities, especially power-reversal games where I pretended to be weaker and a bit scared of him. I also spent time paying attention to him while he played, and he often brought up the theme of his experience in his play. As a result of this, he was able to go back to school the following week without fear and with clear boundaries in his mind if anything similar ever happened again.

Teachers can also use playful approaches to help children in their classrooms feel less stressed. Nathalie Trudel, an early childhood educator in China who works with children aged two to six, described how she used a type of play called "separation games" to help the children in her class cope with the separation from their parents and adjust to the unfamiliar environment at the beginning of a school year:

> I use separation games at the beginning of the school year. We play hide-and-seek to help the children explore the classroom, but more importantly, to alleviate the stress of separation from their families.

Rico Heinisch shared a playful approach he used to help the six-year-old children in his class adapt to the stress of new rules and expectations at the beginning of their first school year. In Aware Parenting, the term "nonsense play" is used for this type of play:

> During the enrollment of the new first grade children at our school, we explained the school rules, and we also

gave the children additional nonsense rules. The children laughed heartily. A year later, at the start of the next school year, they still remembered some of them. Here are a few examples of our nonsense rules:

- Children are not allowed to eat the books.
- Children are not allowed to make themselves invisible.
- No one is allowed to take the school building home on Friday afternoon.
- Walking on the ceiling with shoes is prohibited.

Helping children recover from stress or trauma

- Create emotional safety.
- Allow children to express their emotions through crying.
- Encourage therapeutic play.

Additional tips for supporting children with homework

Earlier in this chapter, I included examples of helping children cope with the stress of homework by supporting their tears. In this section, I share some additional tips for helping children with homework, which can be a source of tension and conflicts between parents and children. As mentioned in Chapter 4, there is no evidence that homework has any educational benefits for children under the age of ten to twelve. Nevertheless, most public schools assign homework to young children, which can put parents in a difficult position.

Young children under ten or twelve cannot be expected to take full responsibility for homework, so it becomes the parents' job to make sure it gets done. Even after children are old enough to assume more responsibility for homework, they may resist doing it. If your children have homework, you may wonder what your role should be and how you can help them complete their assignments without resorting to punishments or rewards.

When my children chose to attend a traditional school (at age ten for my son and age nine for my daughter), I warned them that they would have homework, tests, and grades, which they had never had before. I also let them know that I would not force them to do their homework. However, I explained that they might face consequences at school if they chose not to complete their assignments. Throughout their school career, they both took responsibility for keeping track of their homework and doing it on time.

There is an important difference between *forcing* your children to do homework and *supporting* them in the ways they request. Although I never told my children to do their homework, I *did* offer to help them, and I tried to be available every day. Helping children with homework does not mean doing it for them. Each day, when they returned from school, I asked them if they needed my help with homework, and I let them know when I was available. Sometimes they needed explanations to help them understand a concept. Other times, they wanted help reviewing material for a test. At their request, I taught them some study skills, such as breaking large projects into manageable tasks and completing a little bit each day. When they felt frustrated or overwhelmed, they often needed emotional support, which usually involved me listening supportively while they cried (as described in the previous section).

Sometimes children just need to complain about homework and vent their frustration. At 21 years old, my grandson recalled the following memory of a frustrating homework assignment from his childhood:

> I remember one time, when I was about ten years old, there was a particular homework assignment that I got really upset about. It was a worksheet, and I had to write some things about each topic. It took me a very long time because I had to write neatly, which always took me for-

ever. Also, that particular assignment really annoyed me because it felt very useless. It just felt like busywork. I think I had a tantrum while doing it, at one point, and I wanted to rip it up. I had finished the whole assignment, but I still wanted to rip it up. My mother suggested that I should rip up a copy instead of the real worksheet that I had already completed. So, I made a photocopy, which I ripped up, and then I turned in the original worksheet at school the following day.

It is important for children to have time to relax and play after a full day of school. Even if they have several hours of homework to complete, they will be more willing and able to complete it if they first have freedom to do what they enjoy.

There is no reason why children should be isolated in their rooms while doing homework, unless they choose to be alone. My children each had their own room with a desk, but they rarely chose to study there. Instead, they preferred to work at the dining room table, where they could be near other family members. This was never a problem for me if they cleared the table before mealtimes, which they willingly did.

Resistance to homework does not mean that children lack interest in learning. It simply means that they are not interested in studying that specific topic at that time or in that way. Also, they may be too tired after a long school day. Rather than forcing children to do their homework (which would require an authoritarian approach), I recommend offering help and finding ways to connect the homework to their interests. You can also try to make it playful and fun while using an approach that aligns with their strengths or preferred learning style.

For example, if your son must learn a list of spelling words, you can ask him to draw a picture representing each word and write the word on his drawing. This approach will be especially effective if he likes to draw. If he likes to make up stories, you can suggest that he create a story using all the words from the list. You can help him write it down, and he can read it aloud to you or another family member.

If your daughter needs to memorize the multiplication table for a test, you can use examples relating to her interests. If she loves dinosaurs, you can create word problems about them: *A newborn stegosaurus is three feet long, and an adult stegosaurus is six times longer. How long is the adult stegosaurus?* If she enjoys drawing, she can illustrate the problem with pictures of the dinosaurs. If she is a visual/spatial learner who notices colors and patterns, suggest creating a ten-by-ten multiplication chart, using different colors for each column. This visual aid will help her notice number patterns and make memorization easier.

Suggestions for supporting children with homework

- Encourage relaxation and play immediately after school.

- Don't force them to do their homework.

- Offer your help (but don't do it for them).

- Allow them to complain and cry.

- Find ways to connect the homework to their interests.

- Make it playful and fun.

- Use an approach that aligns with their strengths or preferred learning style.

By supporting your children with homework in these ways, you can create moments of fun and connection while helping them learn.

Alternatives to praise, criticism, and corrections

While supporting children to learn, we naturally feel the need to offer some kind of feedback. However, it's important to recognize that certain kinds of comments are not as helpful as we might think and can even discourage children. In this section, I offer suggestions for helpful ways to share feedback with children about their learning.

In Chapter 4, I described the disadvantages of praising children with value judgments, such as calling something "good." Excessive praise can lead to a fear of failure and increase children's anxiety. Furthermore, praise tends to undermine intrinsic motivation, because it *changes the reason why children engage in learning.* Instead of studying for the pleasure of learning, it teaches children to study for the sake of receiving praise.

How can we help children learn and feel good about themselves without using praise? It may seem strange or even uncaring to refrain from praising children, but there are many effective ways to encourage them and strengthen their self-esteem without the use of value judgments. The following chart offers some alternatives to praise.

How to encourage children without value judgments

- Mirror your children's excitement and pride about their accomplishments. Celebrate with them but avoid value judgments.
  "Wow! You only got one wrong!"
  "It looks like you have learned a lot!"
  "It's fun to know how to do that, isn't it?"

- Offer feedback by comparing their performance *to their own past performance* (but not to others or an arbitrary standard of perfection).
  "That's the longest book you've ever read."

"That's the tallest tower you've ever built."
"That's the farthest you've ever swum!"

- **Share your feelings (be honest and authentic).**
  "Your description of the house makes it easy for me to imagine it."
  "Your drawing reminds me of a warm, summer day."
  "I remember struggling to learn long division at your age."

- **Show interest by asking questions about their feelings.**
  "What was the hardest (or easiest) part of the test?"
  "How do you feel about your grade?"
  "What did you most enjoy in that class? What did you learn?"

- **Provide nonverbal appreciation and encouragement.**
  Watch and listen attentively when they play a musical instrument.
  Take a picture or record them doing something (with their permission)
  Display their artwork on the wall.

In Chapter 4, I also described the potential problems associated with correcting children. While corrections can sometimes help children learn, especially if they have asked for feedback, unsolicited corrections can have the opposite effect. They may make children feel criticized, lower their self-esteem, and create anxiety about trying new things.

It's possible to give helpful feedback to children without directly correcting mistakes. For instance, if a child makes an error while solving a math problem, we might be tempted to point it out immediately. However, it might be more helpful to say, "I'm curious to know how you got your answer. Could you explain the steps you went through?" This approach encourages children to share their thinking, and by doing so, they might discover and correct their own mistakes. They will also feel better about themselves than if we say, "You did that problem wrong."

In schools, some teachers let children work on math problems with peers in small groups, where they can compare answers and identify mistakes together. In this way, children can learn from each other. The teachers are available to help with disagreements that the children cannot resolve by themselves.

Some mistakes don't need to be corrected at all. When children write stories, for example, pointing out spelling errors or imperfect handwriting is usually unhelpful. This type of feedback may discourage them from writing. Instead, we can show interest in their story and make the kind of comments suggested in the previous chart.

Avoiding corrections can also be helpful when children are learning life skills. The following example, shared by one of my clients, illustrates how she refrained from correcting her son when he was learning to help with household chores:

> When my son was small, he had real, child-sized cleaning equipment, and we always cleaned together. I never corrected him or re-did his work because I had read about this approach before he reached that age, and I really resonated with that advice. This gave him a sense of competence and contribution.

Coping with your own feelings

As parents, your emotions can interfere with your ability to support your children in the most helpful ways. It's only natural to feel impatient or frustrated when a child arrives home from school full of anger or resists doing homework. You might feel confused about how to respond without making the problem worse. If your child's school-related struggles remind you of painful experiences from your own childhood, those past traumas may be triggered, affecting your ability to think clearly and respond supportively. For example, your child's low grade or test score could remind you of your own past failures. Additionally, your child's difficulties or resistance to homework might raise genuine concerns about your child's future.

If you frequently lose patience with your children, the first step is to acknowledge your feelings and recognize that they may be connected to your own past. You may find it helpful to explore your own painful learning experiences and express your emotions with someone who will listen without judgment. The exercises at the end of this book suggest topics and questions to explore in this way.

Depending on your children's age, it might also be helpful to share some of your own painful learning experiences with them. For example, if you tell your children about a failed test or a bad grade you received, they may not feel so bad when they experience something similar. It can also help them understand why their own academic struggles affect you so deeply. However, it's important to avoid burdening your children with too much information about your past traumatic experiences, because they may feel that you are too overwhelmed to support them with their own emotions.

Supporting children when they cry can be difficult, especially if you were not allowed to cry as a child. Even though I understood the importance of crying (and had already written books about it) when my children first began experiencing school-related stress, there were times when I still felt impatient with them. When they cried and complained about the amount of homework they had, I often felt like saying, "You could have finished it by now if you hadn't spent so much time complaining!" I never actually said that, but I frequently felt a strong urge to do so.

Supporting children through play and laughter can also be challenging. Many people underestimate the power of play and assume that it's a waste of time. However, it's important to remember that play is never a waste of time, and neither the learning process nor the healing process needs to be serious. Play and laughter can be highly effective tools for helping children learn and also cope with stress.

You might also find it difficult to support your child's learning without relying on praise or constantly correcting their mistakes. It's natural to feel that giving praise and making corrections is an essential part of your role as a parent. However, I encourage you to experiment with some of the alternative approaches described in this chapter. You may find that these methods foster a more positive learning experience for both you and your child.

Chapter 6

Understanding Learning Difficulties

> *"It is standard practice in many schools to punish children for
> tantrums, spacing out, or aggressive outbursts—all of which
> are often symptoms of traumatic stress. When that happens,
> the school, instead of offering a safe haven, becomes
> yet another traumatic trigger."*
> —Bessel van der Kolk

THIS CHAPTER explores the reasons for difficulties that can
interfere with children's ability to learn. I begin by distinguishing
between biological and psychological causes of learning difficulties.
I then explore the psychological causes for challenging behaviors
that children may exhibit in school, and I offer suggestions for
addressing these problems without punishments or rewards.

Biological versus psychological causes
Biological causes
The biological causes of learning challenges include physical disabilities such as blindness or deafness, neurological conditions
present at birth, and brain injury (before or after birth) resulting from accidents, tumors, strokes, malnutrition, drugs, or toxins.
Examples of learning difficulties with identifiable biological causes
include Down syndrome, neuronal migration disorders, fetal alco-
hol syndrome, and many other conditions. Additionally, research
suggests that some cases of autism have a biological basis (a genetic
mutation). To help children with these conditions reach their full

potential, early interventions and appropriate accommodations in school can be beneficial. Some children may need to attend specialized schools or classrooms with teachers trained to meet their particular needs.

I recommend a thorough medical assessment for any child who shows developmental delays or struggles in school. If no obvious medical cause is found, all children should be screened for dyslexia. Research indicates that dyslexia has a biological (genetic) basis and tends to run in families. Children with dyslexia struggle with reading but often excel in other subjects, which is one reason why their dyslexia is often overlooked and not properly diagnosed. Current estimates suggest that about 20% of children have some form of dyslexia, and it is now considered a learning *difference* rather than a disorder.

Children with other inherited traits may also have special educational needs. Some children are more sensitive than others and can become easily overwhelmed by excessive stimulation. Others may be highly gifted in mathematics, music, or drawing and may benefit from special kinds of stimulation or instruction.

It is beyond the scope of this book to discuss educational approaches for all the conditions that result in special educational needs. However, there are excellent resources available for parents. If your child has a special condition, I encourage you to educate yourself and search for the most appropriate learning environment. This might include a traditional public school with accommodations, a private school, a specialized school designed for children with that condition, private tutoring, homeschooling, or a combination of these options. Keep in mind that the best educational setting may change as your child grows older. Most importantly, seek emotional support for yourself. You will probably find it helpful to connect with other parents whose children have similar conditions.

Psychological causes
The psychological causes for learning difficulties include children's cumulative experiences since conception, including the type

of stimulation and discipline received, as well as the amount of stress or trauma to which they have been exposed. To fully understand children's behavior, we cannot ignore these factors. Research indicates that stress and emotional trauma have a huge impact on children's behavior and ability to learn. Recognizing the effects of stress and trauma and understanding how children can recover opens up new possibilities for supporting children with behavioral or learning challenges.

Even when there is a clear biological cause (such as a genetic mutation), environmental factors like stress or trauma can further contribute to a child's difficulties. For instance, children with the biological conditions listed above may become easily frustrated or overwhelmed *because of* the challenges they face. Also, they may be more vulnerable to abuse or bullying, especially if their behavior or appearance differs from that of other children, further adding to their stress. Because of these complex interactions between genetic and environmental factors, it is often difficult to determine the root cause of a child's learning or behavioral difficulties.

Distinguishing between permanent and temporary conditions

Conditions caused by identifiable biological factors (such as genetic mutations or brain injury) are likely to be permanent. Similarly, traits with high heritability (such as dyslexia, high sensitivity, and exceptional talents in specific areas) are also likely to persist as children grow older, even if no specific biological test exists to diagnose them. Those traits reflect natural variations in human neurology (neurodiversity). On the other hand, behaviors and learning difficulties caused primarily by psychological factors are more likely to be temporary conditions, which may improve with psychotherapy, environmental changes, or adjustments in teaching approaches.

When discussing children with learning challenges, it's important to be aware of the underlying assumptions associated with different terms. Psychiatric diagnoses are based entirely on behavioral observations (rather than biological tests) and do not provide information about the underlying cause. Unfortunately, such diagnoses can lead parents to believe that the child was born with a defective brain, which may not be true. The behaviors on which these diagnoses are based could be temporary manifestations of stress or trauma (as explained in Chapter 4).

The term "neurodiverse" can also be misleading. It is commonly used to describe children with a range of conditions and behaviors, regardless of the underlying cause. I avoid using the term because it implies that those behaviors *always* stem from a neurological cause and that the condition is permanent, which may not always be the case.

Nevertheless, identifying and describing children who struggle to learn can be useful. If a child is not developing, behaving, or learning in a typical way for their age, this could indicate a problem for which early interventions could be beneficial. When there is no clear biological cause, I prefer to describe the child's behavior rather than use a diagnostic label, while keeping in mind that the underlying cause could be purely psychological. For instance, I would say that a child has difficulty paying attention in school instead of using a psychiatric label or the term "neurodiverse." This purely descriptive approach makes no assumption about the underlying cause. Instead, it encourages a search for all possible contributing factors, including the child's past experiences, trauma history, and current environment.

A diagnosis of ADHD (attention deficit hyperactivity disorder) can be used to illustrate the complexity of these factors. The behaviors that lead to an ADHD diagnosis have at least three possible causes: prenatal brain injury (perhaps from maternal drug use), a natural variation in inherited traits, or stress and trauma. This third possibility is often overlooked, even though the symptoms of ADHD are the same as typical posttraumatic symptoms (hyperactivity, impulsive behavior, and difficulty paying attention).

Possible causes of behaviors leading to an ADHD diagnosis

• Prenatal brain injury
• Natural variation in inherited traits
• Current stress or unhealed trauma

Before assuming that a child has an irreversible brain disorder, it is important to consider other possible causes for the child's behavior. Even when observable differences in brain function exist, those differences merely reflect *how children are using their brains*. They don't prove that the cause is biological. Since the brain develops in response to experiences, differences in brain function do not necessarily indicate brain damage or an inherited neurological disorder.

There is no doubt that human beings are a neurodiverse species, and each child has a unique neurological profile. However, it's important to remember that a child's nervous system is shaped by both biological *and* psychological factors. When the psychological factors are addressed through psychotherapy, environmental changes, or adjustments in the teaching approach, children's behavior can change, and they may no longer meet the criteria for a psychiatric diagnosis.

In summary, not all behavior problems or learning difficulties are permanent conditions. I avoid using psychiatric labels and the term "neurodiverse" because they imply that children with non-typical behaviors have a permanent neurological condition. This assumption can cause parents and teachers to overlook possible psychological factors contributing to a child's behavior. Considering all possible causes of children's behavior can lead to more effective support strategies. The following section explores possible psychological causes of children's learning challenges.

Psychological causes of common behaviors that can interfere with learning

All children who struggle in school should be screened for dyslexia and neurological disorders that might be contributing factors. If those factors have been ruled out, it's possible that psychological factors lie at the root of a child's difficulties. In this section, I describe five challenging behaviors that parents and teachers might encounter during learning situations, and I explore the possible psychological reasons for these behaviors. I also offer some suggestions for addressing each of these challenges.

Children who resist going to school

It may be difficult for some children to explain why they don't want to go to school. Before assuming that something is wrong with your child, you can explore all the sources of school stress. The problem could simply be that the school's approach to learning does not meet your child's need for play and self-directed learning.

Your child's school resistance may have nothing to do with the teaching approach. Maybe your child has been bullied or encountered racist or sexist comments. Hearing about school shootings or terrorist attacks can also contribute to children's anxiety and reluctance to attend school.

I recommend visiting the school with your child, if possible, and observing their behavior in that environment. You might notice something that explains their reluctance to be there. For example, there could be a lot of noise or an aggressive classmate. You could also discuss the problem and possible solutions with your child's teacher, who might have helpful insights and suggestions.

I also suggest engaging your child in role-play at home with a school theme. You could play the role of a student while your child pretends to be the teacher and then reverse the roles. Children often bring up conflicts and painful emotions through play, and this might give you some clues about why your child refuses to go to school. Role play can also be therapeutic, especially if you follow your child's lead.

If you think your child is struggling with deeper emotions caused by a traumatic experience or fear of school shootings, you can offer support by encouraging them to express those emotions by talking, crying, or through therapeutic play. Your child might also benefit from professional therapy with someone trained in treating childhood trauma and anxiety. The following chart summarizes several reasons for school resistance.

Possible reasons for school resistance

- The school does not meet the child's needs for play and self-directed learning.

- The child does not feel safe at school because of teasing, bullying, or abuse.

- The child does not feel safe at school because of racism or sexism.

- The child does not feel safe at school for other reasons (e.g. fear of a school shooting).

- The child is too young to be away from the parents for a full day.

- The child is highly sensitive and finds the school environment overstimulating.

- The child has separation anxiety because a parent is ill.

- The child has separation anxiety because of past separation trauma.

- The teacher has criticized or humiliated the child.

- The child is struggling to learn and feels incompetent.

There could be other reasons, but this section describes only possible *psychological* reasons, with the assumption that dyslexia and neurological disorders have been ruled out.

If your child's school resistance continues despite your efforts to address the underlying cause, you might consider a different school or homeschooling.

Children who daydream and have trouble paying attention

Children who daydream frequently often disconnect from their surroundings, fail to pay attention to the teacher, or stop focusing on their schoolwork. This inattention can interfere with their ability to concentrate and learn in a classroom setting.

Boredom can lead to daydreaming. Children who already know the material being taught might lose interest and begin to think about other things. Introducing more stimulating activities could be helpful. On the other hand, daydreaming can also occur when the material is too difficult.

Another reason for attention problems is that the subject being taught does not interest the child. Following a child's interests can be beneficial, but this is not always possible or practical in schools with a preset curriculum. Furthermore, some subjects (such as multiplication tables) are essential for children to learn, even if they lack the motivation to do so. If the topic doesn't interest the child, a teaching approach that incorporates their interests or strengths can be helpful (as described in the previous chapter).

Children might also stop paying attention when the teaching approach does not match their learning style. For example, visual learners might "zone out" while a teacher is talking, especially if they have poor auditory learning skills. Using images or diagrams can help capture such children's attention.

Some children become inattentive when there is too much stimulation. This situation is the opposite of boredom and is more likely to occur with highly sensitive children, who become easily overwhelmed by excessive sensory input. When they begin to feel overstimulated, they simply stop paying attention. Providing breaks from stimulation or a quiet area in a classroom can be beneficial for highly sensitive children.

Current stress or unhealed trauma from the past can also contribute to daydreaming and attention problems. When children feel anxious or unsafe, their ability to focus decreases. Children who daydream and who have trouble paying attention in school may be in a state of mild dissociation, which is a common post-traumatic symptom (as explained in Chapter 4). Dissociation is a deceptively calm state, characterized by emotional numbness. Although these children might appear relaxed, dissociation is different from true relaxation. From an evolutionary point of view, it makes little sense for children to prioritize learning when their brains are focused on safety and survival. These children would benefit from emotional support based on the healing approaches described in Chapter 5.

Before assuming that a child has trouble paying attention, it's important to interpret their behavior correctly. For instance, some

Possible reasons for daydreaming and attention problems

- The child is bored.

- The topic does not interest the child.

- The teaching style does not work well for the child.

- The child is highly sensitive and finds the school environment overstimulating.

- The child does not feel safe at school.

- The child is preoccupied by stress at home.

- The child is in a state of mild dissociation due to unhealed trauma.

children look at the ceiling or even close their eyes when they are thinking about a math problem or figuring out what to write. Teachers might misinterpret that behavior as daydreaming or inattention when, in fact, the child is deep in concentration.

Children who are agitated or hyperactive

Children who are agitated and hyperactive can't sit still for long periods. Like those who daydream frequently, they often have difficulty paying attention in school and cannot concentrate on one thing for very long.

Hyperactivity may be a response to boredom, which can arise when children already understand the material, lack interest in the topic, or find that the teaching approach doesn't align with their learning style. Rather than daydreaming, as described in the previous section, some children respond in the opposite way by becoming more physically active to generate more interesting sensory stimulation.

Agitation and hyperactivity could also indicate a naturally high energy level and a legitimate need to be active. If movement is the underlying need, these children might pay better attention if they can move their bodies or do something with their hands. A helpful approach would be to incorporate movement into the learning process. Tactile experiences with sand, clay, water, or finger paints can also help agitated children calm down and begin to focus.

Another possible cause of hyperactive behavior is current stress or unhealed trauma from the past. As explained in Chapter 4, hyperarousal is a common post-traumatic symptom characterized by alertness and preparation for fight or flight. It differs from the calm state typical of dissociation, but neither post-traumatic condition is conducive to learning. As with children who daydream and can't pay attention because of dissociation, hyperactive children would benefit from emotional support based on the healing approaches described in Chapter 5.

Possible reasons for agitation and hyperactivity

• The child is bored.

• The topic does not interest the child.

• The teaching style does not work well for the child.

• The child has a legitimate need for body movement.

• The child is feeling stressed or unsafe.

• The child is in a state of hyperarousal from unhealed trauma.

Children who show little interest in learning

Children are born with a strong motivation to learn. When they appear unmotivated, they are probably resisting *what* or *how* they are being taught rather than resisting learning itself. The following guidelines can increase children's interest and motivation: follow their interests, use playful teaching methods, and adapt to their preferred learning style. These are the same guidelines for parents mentioned in Chapter 5 for supporting children with homework.

All children are interested in *something*. Some may enjoy cooking, while others are fascinated by volcanoes or curious about birds. Parents can easily provide stimulation and learning opportunities at home that relate to their children's interests, as described in previous chapters. Teachers can also look for ways to incorporate children's interests into their lessons, although this can be challenging within a predetermined curriculum.

Before assuming that a child lacks motivation, it's important to consider other factors, such as past experiences of humiliation or criticism. Additionally, family stress or trauma can also contribute to apparent lack of interest in learning.

Attempts to motivate children with grades, verbal praise, or other kinds of rewards will not increase their interest in learning. Instead, those external motivators may have the opposite effect by causing stress and by also decreasing intrinsic motivation. (Please see Chapters 4 and 8 for more information about the disadvantages of rewards.)

Possible reasons for lack of interest in learning

• The topic does not interest the child.

• The teaching style does not work well for the child.

• The child is preoccupied by family stress.

• The child has given up trying to learn because of humiliation or criticism.

• The child's intrinsic motivation has decreased because of grades or rewards.

Children who resist being told what to do

Some children refuse to follow instructions or do what adults tell them to do. When this refusal occurs in learning situations, parents and teachers may understandably lose patience. Several reasons may explain why children refuse to comply.

Perhaps these children have not been given enough choices, freedom, or autonomy in the past. Maybe they feel rebellious because they have previously experienced punishment for disobedience. Their hesitation to follow directions at school could also stem from past failures.

Some children resist instructions because they don't fully understand them and need more guidance. Others may resist because they lack sufficient time for free play.

Family stress can also contribute to non-compliance. Major life changes, such as the birth of a baby, parental conflicts or divorce, health issues, or financial struggles, can leave children feeling emotionally overwhelmed.

Nathalie Trudel described a child in her class who refused to follow instructions:

> One day, there was a child in my class (age five) who refused to cooperate or follow instructions. I asked her to stay after class so I could talk to her. After class, I sat with her and asked her what was going on. It was a Monday, and I know that students bring stress from home into the classroom, so I asked about her weekend. She told me that she went to the hospital to visit her grandfather, who was gravely ill. Her mother had told her that Grandpa was probably going to die, and the nurses would not be able to fix him. I asked her how she felt about her grandfather being sick. She said that she was sad, and her mother was also sad. They had cried together about it the day before. I asked her if she wanted a hug, and she said yes, so I opened my arms offering comfort. I told her that even if her grandfather died, he would still be with her in her heart. She leaned in for another hug, this time putting her full weight into it. When she pulled away, she had tears in her eyes. I told her that I would be available to her any time she wanted.

It is never helpful to use threats, bribes, or punishment to force children to obey. Authoritarian approaches may result in short-term compliance but can lead to anger and resentment and can interfere with children's ability to concentrate and learn. Furthermore, even if we can force children to follow instructions, *we can never force them to learn*. For learning to be effective, children must *be willing* to learn.

Possible reasons for non-compliance

- The child has a legitimate need for freedom, choice, and autonomy.

- The child is rebelling against punitive parenting or teaching.

- The child is afraid of failure.

- The child needs more instructions or guidance.

- The child needs more time for free play.

- The child is preoccupied with family stress.

In the past, parents and teachers were led to believe that children with the behaviors described in this chapter needed to be "disciplined." Those who had difficulty concentrating were told to stop daydreaming and pay attention. Those who were hyperactive were told to sit still. Those who disobeyed were punished, while those who sat quietly in their seats and followed instructions were praised and rewarded.

Nowadays, many people assume that children with these behaviors suffer from psychiatric disorders and need medication. I am not opposed to medication that meets a genuine medical need. However, I question the use of psychiatric medication simply to change a child's behavior, especially before making efforts to modify the child's environment or explore all possible contributing factors.

In Aware Parenting, we avoid the use of punishments and rewards. Instead, we look for all the possible underlying reasons for children's behavior. When we become aware of their feelings and needs, we can often find effective solutions without punishments, rewards, or psychiatric medication. I recommend considering all the possible factors discussed in this chapter, which are summarized in the following chart.

Summary of reasons why some children struggle in school or are difficult to teach

Possible biological reasons

- The child has a physical disability (such as blindness or deafness).
- The child is experiencing illness, pain, hunger, or fatigue.
- The child has a genetic neurological disorder.
- The child has brain damage.
- The child is dyslexic.
- The child is highly sensitive.

Possible psychological reasons

- The child has separation anxiety.
- The child does not feel safe.
- The child is preoccupied with family stress.
- The child is overstimulated.
- The child is bored.
- The child has been criticized or humiliated.
- The child has received a bad grade and feels incompetent.
- The child is afraid of failure.
- The child is afraid of punishment.
- The child has been teased, bullied, or excluded.
- The child has experienced sexism or racism.
- The topic does not interest the child.
- The teaching style does not work well for the child.

- The child does not understand the instructions.
- The child needs more guidance.
- The child is in a state of dissociation (due to unhealed trauma).
- The child is in a state of hyperarousal (due to unhealed trauma).
- The child has a legitimate need for body movement.
- The child has a legitimate need for freedom, choice, or autonomy.
- The child has a legitimate need for play and social interaction.
- The child has a legitimate need for attention.

I would like to end this chapter with the story of a child who attended the same alternative school as my children (described in Chapter 1):

Susan's parents enrolled her in the alternative program when she was seven years old. She had learned to read but had trouble sitting still. She was constantly moving and talking with other children and had been diagnosed with ADHD while attending her previous school. Her doctor recommended psychiatric medication, but her parents chose not to give it to her. Instead, they removed her from the traditional public school she had been attending and transferred her to the alternative program. Susan was a highly creative and social child. She thrived in the alternative program, where she was not required to sit still for long periods. She spent most of her time using the craft materials, playing, and interacting with other children. She quickly made many friends and emerged as a natural leader. When she was eleven years old, she wrote a play and recruited several of her classmates to perform it with her. In addition to an engaging plot, her play included songs and dances, which she composed and choreographed herself. The performance took place at the end-of-year celebration in the school theater, with all the children's family members in the audience. No adults assisted with rehearsals or the final production. Susan enjoyed her multiple roles as author, composer, choreographer, costume designer, director, actor, and dancer. She never took psychiatric medication.

In this example, Susan needed to be active and move her body because of her strong kinesthetic intelligence. She also displayed high interpersonal intelligence (social skills). In a traditional classroom, she was not free to move or talk with other children as much as she wanted. In the alternative program, however, she was free to move around and interact with other children most of the time.

As mentioned earlier, a psychiatric diagnosis does not always indicate a neurological disorder. In Susan's case, she flourished without medication. It is important to remember that ADHD is simply a descriptive label based on a behavioral checklist. As explained at the beginning of this chapter, the behaviors associated with an ADHD diagnosis can stem from multiple causes, and there is not necessarily anything wrong with the child's brain.

Most children thrive in nonpunitive learning environments that provide choices, opportunities to learn by discovery, and freedom of movement, without the stress of tests, grades, or homework. However, changing the environment may not be sufficient for every child. Some might require additional support or specialized teaching approaches.

For example, dyslexic children may avoid trying to read because it's not easy for them. They can benefit from gentle encouragement and dyslexic-specific instruction designed to help them overcome their specific learning difficulties.

Similarly, stressed and traumatized children may also need additional support. In the alternative school that my children attended, some children came from stressful home environments or had experienced trauma. For these children, a stress-free, alternative learning environment was not enough, because they needed additional emotional support.

Chapter 7

Types of Schools

> *"More important than the curriculum is the question
> of the methods of teaching and the spirit in
> which teaching is given."*
> —Bertrand Russell

IN THIS CHAPTER, I begin with a brief history of schools
and educational reformers in Europe and North America. I then
describe the most well-known school options, focusing on their
characteristics and major advantages. In the final section, I discuss
homeschooling and include advice from three Aware Parenting
instructors who homeschooled their children. Children can thrive
in all these learning environments. However, painful experiences
(such as those described in Chapter 4) can also occur in any setting,
regardless of teachers' good intentions.

A brief history of schools and educational reformers
Throughout history, schools have served a variety of purposes. One
function has been to train children to become religious leaders
capable of reading and interpreting sacred texts. Schools have
taught literacy and computational skills to support governmental
administration, conduct commerce, and record important events
for future generations. Additionally, they have trained children to
follow orders, preparing them to become obedient citizens who
could work in factories or serve in the military. Another key func-

tion has been to provide supervised care for children while their parents worked.

Sadly, in colonized countries, schools have often been used as agents of oppression, forcing indigenous children to adopt the colonizers' language, religion, and customs. In the United States and Canada, for example, Native American children were removed from their families and forced to attend boarding schools, where they were forbidden from speaking their native languages.

Today, many people assume that the primary purpose of schools is to teach children the skills necessary for earning a living and filling the jobs needed by society. The goal is to train children to become informed citizens capable of keeping the culture functioning, whether by running farms and factories, engaging in commerce, constructing stable buildings, or providing medical care.

However, some people believe that schools have a broader purpose: to help children understand the world, become innovative problem-solvers, make scientific discoveries, and contribute to a better world. Ever since the beginning of universal public schooling, educational pioneers and reformers have had this broader vision in mind, and they have recognized that a different teaching approach is necessary to reach such goals. They have proposed methods that go beyond, or completely replace, traditional approaches based on direct instruction.

In Europe, these attempts to reform education began long before Jean Piaget studied how children learn. These pioneers and reformers include John Amos Comenius (in what is now the Czech Republic), Jean-Jacques Rousseau and Johann Heinrich Pestalozzi (in Switzerland), Friedrich Fröbel (in Germany), Rudolf Steiner (in Germany and Switzerland, originally from Austria), Maria Montessori (in Italy), Janusz Korczak (in Poland), Alexander Sutherland Neill (in England), and Célestin Freinet (in France).

In North America as well, despite the strong influence of behaviorism on education, several pioneers and reformers have proposed alternatives to traditional schooling. Many were influenced by Piaget's work or by the European reformers. These American and Canadian reformers include Mary Peabody, Francis Parker, John Dewey, Jerome Bruner, John Holt, David Elkind, Daniel Greenberg, Eleanor Duckworth, Herbert Kohl, Howard Gardner, Peter Gray, Thomas Armstrong, and Alfie Kohn.

Many of these European and North American reformers have inspired alternative educational movements and schools worldwide. Some of their ideas and methods have also influenced mainstream public education. Teacher training programs for public schools often include a variety of approaches, some of which are based on these reformers' ideas. More information about each of these reformers can be found in the Appendix.

In most countries, some kind of schooling is mandatory, and government-funded public education usually begins between the ages of four and seven. The assumption is that children require formal instruction starting at this age. Before children reach school age, however, the educational options are more likely to include learning environments that encourage free play, choice, and hands-on learning by discovery.

In the United States, for instance, the National Association for the Education of Young Children has established guidelines for best teaching practices in early childhood education. Their guidelines align with the principles of learning described in this book. However, once children reach the age of mandatory schooling, public education in most countries (including the United States) still relies heavily on direct instruction, tests, grades, and other traditional approaches.

Two types of goals

The type of education that you offer your children depends on your goals. Like most parents, I wanted my children to learn how to read and write, develop basic math skills, and gain knowledge in history, geography, and science. I also wanted them to develop expertise in specific fields, learn to use technology, and eventually choose a career that would allow them to earn a living.

However, like the educational reformers described in the previous section, I had additional goals. I wanted my children to maintain their innate curiosity and love of learning, to be creative and innovative thinkers, to ask meaningful questions, and to know where to find answers. I hoped they would develop good communication and social skills and show respect for people who were different from themselves. I wanted them to pursue their interests, reach their full potential, and choose a profession that they would enjoy.

Perhaps most importantly, I wanted them to have high self-esteem and confidence in their ability to master whatever they chose to learn, whether it was playing a musical instrument, computer programming, or cooking. I hoped that they would become competent, joyful, and lifelong learners.

If your only goal is to raise children who become proficient enough in specific subjects to earn a living and carry on the culture they were born into, you may think that a traditional approach based on direct instruction, memorization, and drill is appropriate and sufficient. This approach sees children as empty vessels to be filled with knowledge. For this approach to work, however, it requires authoritarian control and coercion, because children usually find such teaching methods boring and even stressful.

If you have additional goals, as I did, to raise children to be creative thinkers who maintain their natural curiosity and motivation, a different approach is needed. The method must align more closely with children's natural learning processes by allowing them to follow their interests and learn by discovery. The emphasis will need to be more on encouraging them to think and solve problems instead of forcing them to memorize facts and do repetitive rote work. With this approach, rewards and punishments become unnecessary, because children naturally enjoy learning in these ways.

My basic assumption is that this second approach to education is the best way to reach both goals, and it's also better for the future of the world. We are faced with many problems that affect all of us, and we need to raise children who will have the courage, determination, knowledge, creativity, motivation, and skills to find solutions. How can we feed a growing world population? What can we do about climate change? How can we prevent child abuse? What are the root causes of terrorism? Is there a cure for cancer? How can we help people suffering from chronic depression? To solve these kinds of problems, we need an educational approach that goes beyond the acquisition of basic skills and facts. From the very start, we must emphasize thinking and creative problem-solving.

School options

After you have clarified your goals, your choice of school for your children will depend on the types of schools available, your children's specific educational needs, and your financial resources. While considering your school choices, keep in mind that the most important factor is often the teacher. All teachers, no matter how well-trained or well-intentioned, are inevitably influenced by their past experiences. Their interpretation and implementation of the school's philosophy depend on their own schooling experience, stress levels, and trauma history. The schools described in this chapter may have highly empathic and patient teachers. On the other hand, the teachers could be well-intentioned but lacking in empathy or patience.

Even if you are not entirely comfortable with any of these options, remember that you, the parents, are even more influential than your children's teachers or the type of school they attend. You can help your children cope with school-related stress and supplement their education with the information and values you provide at home. Children can learn in any of these school settings, but parents remain the most significant factor in their education.

Note: This section is for informational purposes only. I do not endorse any specific kind of school, nor is this a comprehensive list. I have included only the most common school options.

Traditional public schools

The approach to public education differs considerably between and within countries, but there are some commonalities in public education around the world.

A major advantage of public schools is that they are usually free (or low cost). They provide supervised environments for children during the day, which allows parents to hold jobs outside the home without having to pay for childcare. They are usually located near students' homes, which allows children to walk or ride a bicycle to school. If the schools are further away, free bus transportation is often available. Neighborhood public schools allow children to make friends with other children who live nearby and to feel part of a neighborhood community.

Another advantage is that public school teachers have received training in child development, teaching methods, and classroom management. These schools often have resources, such as books, art supplies, science equipment, and computers, which may be lacking in the homes of children from economically disadvantaged homes. Public schools may also have the necessary resources to develop individualized educational plans for children with special needs.

Alternative schools

Also called non-traditional or progressive schools, a variety of institutions fall into this category. In some countries, they are private, but in others, they receive public funding and operate as alternative programs within public school systems. Alternative schools called "open classrooms" flourished in the United States and in some other countries during the 1960s and 1970s. Two alternative schools gained wide recognition in the twentieth century: Summerhill School in England and Sudbury Valley School in the United States.

Teachers in alternative schools rely less on direct instruction than those in traditional schools. The classrooms often resemble the active, natural learning environments typical of play-based preschools for younger children. The curriculum often stems from the children's interests, and skills like reading, writing, and mathematics are learned in the context of real-life experiences, playful activities, and projects such as cooking, gardening, and field trips.

Alternative schools typically avoid the use of punishment, and, in some cases, also avoid tests, grades, and homework. Children often have opportunities to talk, play, and work with other children of different ages rather than being restricted to their own age group.

Alternative schools can benefit all children, but they may be especially effective for those who quickly lose interest when reading, writing, and math are taught as isolated subjects, disconnected from any meaningful context. They can be a good choice for families who would like to offer their children a non-traditional approach to education but lack the time or desire for homeschooling (or for those living in countries where homeschooling is illegal).

Montessori schools

Maria Montessori, an Italian doctor and educator, started the Montessori school movement. She specialized in psychiatry and pediatrics before turning her interest to education. After observing children in a mental asylum, where they lacked sufficient stimulation, she recognized the importance of a stimulating environment for optimal child development and learning. Her approach was based on the belief that children will naturally choose to engage in activities that foster learning and healthy development when given the freedom to explore in an environment with educational materials.

Montessori classrooms minimize direct instruction, and children learn primarily through discovery during hands-on interactions with specially designed educational materials. The unique Montessori materials stimulate the different senses, encourage children to think and solve problems, and support the learning of reading, writing, mathematics, music, art, science, history, and geography. Most children find them attractive and enjoyable to work with.

Children progress at their own pace without tests or grades.

They are also encouraged to develop independence and practical skills such as setting and clearing the table, putting materials back where they belong, cleaning, and gardening.

In some parts of the world, Montessori schools are private and expensive, but in others, they receive government funding. They can be a good fit for children who enjoy independent learning and who are progressing in some areas more quickly or more slowly than other children their age.

Waldorf (Steiner) schools

Waldorf schools are based on the philosophy of Rudolf Steiner, an Austrian-born philosopher and educational reformer who lived in Germany and Switzerland. He founded anthroposophy, a spiritual and philosophical movement that influenced his educational approach. The first Waldorf school opened in Stuttgart, Germany, in 1919. The movement spread first to the Netherlands and the United Kingdom, then to many other countries around the world. Waldorf education is now the largest independent school movement in the world. In most countries, they are known as Steiner schools.

The Waldorf approach aims to promote children's intellectual, artistic, and practical skills with a focus on imagination and creativity. Imaginative play is encouraged, and the curriculum includes stories, art, music, and real-life activities such as cooking and gardening. Children create and illustrate their own textbooks, even in subjects like mathematics. The teachers respect children's individual learning rates and discourage competition.

The equipment in Waldorf schools is made from natural products such as wood, cloth, and beeswax crayons. Parents are encouraged to avoid screen time for their children at home. Children are not tested or graded until the high school level, and students remain with the same teacher for multiple years, allowing the teachers to develop a deep understanding of each child.

Waldorf schools may be a good fit for families who agree with the underlying spiritual and philosophical beliefs on which they are based. They provide an esthetically pleasant, non-competitive learning environment and may appeal especially to sensitive children with a vivid imagination.

Outdoor schools (also called nature schools or forest schools)

The outdoor school movement began in Scandinavia in the 1950s and has since spread to other countries. Children spend most of their time in natural settings, such as wooded areas. Through observation and exploration, they learn about the natural world, studying plants, animals, rocks, soil, water, pollution, weather, and ecosystems. They develop spatial skills by finding their way through the forest, and they learn basic engineering principles by constructing shelters from natural materials. The teachers often encourage teamwork and cooperative problem-solving, which helps children develop social skills. Mathematics, reading, and writing are usually integrated into nature-based projects rather than taught as separate subjects.

Outdoor schools can be a good fit for children who have difficulty sitting still, those with a strong affinity for nature, or those who become bored with traditional teaching methods.

Homeschooling

Homeschooling is legal in many countries. The main advantage is that parents can offer their children a personalized curriculum by following each child's individual interests, abilities, and learning styles. Homeschooling avoids the stress of homework, tests, grades, and time schedules. It allows parents to connect with their children while exploring topics of interest and engaging in meaningful, enjoyable educational projects and activities. Finally, homeschooling parents can offer their children an emotionally safe learning environment free of pressure, competition, or authoritarian discipline.

Homeschooling parents typically make use of the internet as well as resources in their communities, such as libraries, museums, and experts in specific fields. They often meet with other homeschooling families for social interaction, educational projects, or field trips. These gatherings provide children with opportunities to socialize with other children and adults.

Joss Goulden homeschooled her two children and offered the following words of support and encouragement for homeschooling parents:

> Support yourself to get free from the cultural conditioning about learning and to understand that it is the result of living, not the result of being taught. Value all forms of learning and all types of intelligence equally. Get support to explore and work through your own school trauma and the ways that it still affects you as an adult. Reach out and find ways to build community and connection with others. Find ways to meet your own needs so you will have the capacity to support your children while dealing with the big responsibility of homeschooling. Enjoy the lifelong learning journey together, so you can explore and learn whatever is of interest to you, while you support your children to do the same. Get support for your own feelings that will come up. Remember that children are born to learn and that you don't need to motivate or coerce them to do so. Remember that everything your child does, especially when they choose it themselves, is a natural learning experience. Enjoy the liberation of seeing the world as your classroom and understanding that learning happens everywhere. Reassure yourself that learning is often not linear and is not chopped into discrete subjects like curricula at school. Support your children to heal from stress and trauma and to release feelings that might otherwise get in the way of learning. Remember that many people won't understand or support your choice to homeschool your children. Get support from like-minded families and share your feelings of doubt, worry, or frustration. Remember that you know your children better than anyone else

and that you are the best person in the world to support their learning. You don't need a degree or to be brilliant at mathematics. You just need to be connected and loving with your children while facilitating their exploration of the world and supporting their innate desire to learn.

Marion Rose also homeschooled her two children and shared her experience and advice:

My daughter and son are now young adults, and they didn't ever go to school. It took me many years to get free from my conditioning about school. Over time, I came to value all forms of learning equally, instead of believing that reading and writing are superior. Through observing my children, I came to deeply trust their innate desire for learning and competence. I saw repeatedly that when they were interested in something, they would be willing to immerse themselves in learning it until they had gained deep knowledge or competence. My invitation to you as a homeschooling parent is to focus on two core things: your own de-conditioning in relation to learning, and healing from your own school trauma. This will speed up the process of really being able to trust your children and their innate desire for learning and competence! I invite you to see if you can enjoy the process! I am so incredibly glad that my children did not go to school. I see their curiosity in life, their passion for learning, and their clear thinking every day.

Vivian Viester, the mother of a teenage, homeschooled son, offered the following words of advice:

I would love to encourage you to stay connected with your truth and values. Reach out to other families who are on the same journey and also to those whose children are a few years older. Having a support network can make a big difference. It's also important to have listening support for all the feelings, fears, and worries that may arise on this journey. The more we have our feelings heard, the clearer we can see, and the more connected we can stay with our values. This helps us support our children in the ways we truly want to. Our children have a natural love for learning. They learn some things earlier, others later, but when they need or want to learn something, they will do so easily when they are ready. For parents who homeschool, I encourage you to trust the timing of both your child's learning process and your own timing. Make the best of the resources and moments you have.

Chapter 8

Twelve Principles of Learning

"One test of the correctness of educational procedure is the happiness of the child."
—Maria Montessori

IN THIS CHAPTER, I present twelve principles of learning, which summarize the information from the previous chapters. These principles reflect children's natural learning processes and are supported by numerous studies in psychology, child development, and education. Key research findings are included in this chapter. References for the studies and books relating to each of these principles are provided in the reference section at the back of the book.

Principle 1
All children are born with the desire and ability to learn.

The function of our brain is to learn about the environment and figure out how best to survive in it. Millions of years of human evolution have perfected this learning process, which means that babies are born knowing how to learn and will do so spontaneously. The term "intrinsic motivation" refers to the spontaneous tendency to explore, seek novelty and challenges, exercise one's capacities, and learn. It implies learning for its own sake, as opposed to learning to obtain a reward. All mammals show evidence of intrinsic motivation to explore their environment, practice skills, and strive for mastery.

When we observe babies and toddlers, we can see how motivated they are to develop motor skills. They try repeatedly to grasp objects, roll over, crawl, and walk. They work hard at these skills until they master them. They spontaneously begin to talk, and they persist in perfecting their speech until they can make themselves understood.

Children are naturally curious. When we take toddlers for walks, they stop to inspect flowers and bugs. While shopping with us, they reach out to touch everything in sight. As soon as they develop sufficient language skills, they begin to ask questions. When my son was three years old, he asked questions such as: "Who turned on the rain? Do frogs have mommies? How do trees eat? What happens to my pee when I flush the toilet? When will I know how to read?" When my grandson was only two years old, we watched the sunset together, and he asked, "Why is the sun setting?" There's no doubt that children are naturally curious and eager to learn about their world.

Children constantly assimilate information and acquire new skills, whether we try to teach them or not. In fact, *we cannot prevent children from learning.* They naturally absorb information while exploring everything that their brains and bodies are capable of. The learning process is inherently pleasant, just like all other survival-related activities such as eating. Studies indicate that learning for the pleasure of learning activates the same brain regions and mechanisms associated with satisfying basic needs such as hunger (specifically, the dopaminergic system).

Principle 2
Children learn best when the learning is self-initiated, arising from their own curiosity and interests, rather than imposed on them. They benefit from an approach that allows choices and self-direction.

When we allow children to follow their own interests, they don't need any external motivation to learn because their natural curiosity drives them. Educational approaches based on this principle are known as self-directed learning, which aligns with a motivational theory in psychology called self-determination theory. This theory suggests that children have basic needs that must be met for optimal learning. One of these needs is a sense of autonomy, which is the feeling of being in control. Extensive research supports this theory.

This principle does not imply that we should avoid suggesting topics for children to learn. However, studies have shown that children learn better when teaching methods support their autonomy by allowing them to make some choices about what and how they learn. On the other hand, when teachers discourage choice and self-direction, children lose their motivation to learn.

Principle 3
Children learn best by discovery through hands-on experiences rather than direct verbal instruction. Concept formation and abstract thinking arise naturally from concrete experiences.

Numerous studies confirm that children understand and retain information better when they discover the concepts themselves rather than learning through direct instruction. In fact, many facts and concepts can be learned without any formal instruction at all. However, studies suggest that some guidance can be helpful, and the most effective approach is one that educators and researchers call "guided discovery."

Children's ability to think abstractly and understand symbols, general concepts, and logic develops naturally from earlier, concrete experiences. At birth, babies lack the ability to use symbols and think abstractly. They gain these skills after acquiring an understanding of underlying concepts through direct experience and interactions with the world. Concrete experiences continue to play an important role in learning throughout childhood and even beyond. Teaching symbols before children fully understand the concepts is less effective than first helping children gain direct experience with the concepts.

Principle 4
Play is the primary mode of learning during the first eight to ten years. It has three major functions:
- Play helps children acquire physical, social, and intellectual skills.
- Play helps children learn and assimilate new information.
- Play helps children release stress and work through traumatic experiences.

Discovery learning through concrete experiences is more effective in spontaneous, playful situations than in serious, artificially contrived teaching situations. Play is one of the most important activities during childhood, and much learning occurs during children's free play, which is never a waste of time! Studies have found that learning through play promotes healthy child development, better concentration, and effective learning. Playing with others, whether adults or peers, also helps children develop social skills and improve brain function.

Play is an antidote to stress. Opportunities for free play can enhance children's emotional health and self-confidence. Conversely, a lack of sufficient free play during childhood can contribute to anxiety and depression later in life. In addition, certain types of interactive play between adults and children are highly effective in helping children process emotions and recover from stressful or traumatic experiences. Laughter is a well-documented stress-release mechanism, which is particularly effective in reducing anxiety.

Principle 5

Appropriate stimulation is important. A rich environment with a variety of manipulative materials facilitates children's learning. Children also benefit by being exposed to stories, books, people, animals, natural environments, ideas, music, games, and real-life activities.

Children need stimulation. Studies have shown that children from stimulating home environments perform better in school than those whose homes lack stimulation. In addition to providing books and toys, parents and teachers can enhance children's learning by offering a variety of educational materials, experiences, and ideas.

Children need opportunities to interact with other children and adults not only for play but also to ask questions and learn about other people's behaviors, thoughts, and moods. They also benefit from observing adults engaged in meaningful work so they can learn through imitation. Exposure to nature allows them to learn about plants, animals, and geology. The more children can experience different aspects of the world, the better they will be able to find their place in it and figure out what subjects they want to explore in more depth.

Principle 6

The best toys are ones that inspire children to imagine, build, create, and think.

Toys can be valuable learning tools, especially if they encourage active engagement. When selecting toys for your children, avoid those that provide only passive entertainment. Instead, look for ones that inspire creativity and problem-solving. For example, a set of wooden blocks offers more learning opportunities than a prefabricated castle.

Toys that promote movement are also beneficial. Simple toy cars that children can push around themselves offer more opportunities for movement, active engagement, and creativity than battery-operated vehicles that function by remote control.

Principle 7
Children develop at their own pace and earlier is not necessarily better. It's normal for them to acquire some skills more slowly while they are busy mastering others.

Individual differences in learning rates have both genetic and environmental causes, and there is no evidence that children who acquire skills early are more intelligent than those who develop them later. (For example, Einstein did not begin speaking until he was three years old.)

However, when children have significant difficulties in a specific area, such as reading, compared to other children the same age, it is important to assess them for learning disabilities and neurological problems. Some children have underlying conditions that can interfere with learning, and early interventions can be beneficial.

Principle 8
There are many kinds of intelligence, and it cannot be measured with a single score (such as an IQ test score). Children who are weak in one kind of intelligence may be strong in others. Children can benefit from educational opportunities that help them use and develop all forms of intelligence.

Human beings are neurologically diverse, and the theory of multiple intelligences describes one aspect of this diversity. For example, some children are gifted for mathematics, while others excel in music or art. This theory, supported by neurological, empirical, and evolutionary evidence, initially identified seven types of intelligence: verbal/linguistic, logical/mathematical, visual/spatial, musical, kinesthetic, interpersonal, and intrapersonal. Later, naturalistic intelligence was added to the list. Thomas Armstrong, an expert in this field, uses the following simplified terms: word smart, number smart, picture smart, music smart, body smart, self smart, people smart, and nature smart.

Types of intelligence

- Verbal/linguistic
- Logical/mathematical
- Visual/spatial
- Musical
- Kinesthetic
- Interpersonal
- Intrapersonal
- Naturalistic

Children with strong verbal and mathematical intelligence typically perform well in traditional school settings, where the emphasis is on reading, writing, and mathematics. Children who are weak in these areas often struggle in school and feel stupid. However, they often excel in other areas, such as music, art, sports, or social skills, if given the opportunity.

Children also have different learning styles and preferences for *how* to learn. Several different learning style dimensions have been proposed. One model is based on the eight types of intelligence. Another proposes four contrasting dimensions: active versus reflective, sensing versus intuitive, visual versus verbal, and sequential versus global.

A popular educational theory, known as the "meshing hypothesis," suggests that children learn best when the teaching method matches their individual learning style. For example, to learn about dinosaurs, children with a verbal learning style might prefer reading books or listening to descriptions, while visual learners might benefit more from pictures or from building a three-dimensional model of a dinosaur.

Critics of the meshing hypothesis claim that there is insufficient evidence to support the idea that matching teaching methods to learning styles improves learning outcomes. However, teaching based on the meshing hypothesis may be useful for *motivating* children to learn about subjects in which they have no interest. For instance, children who are naturally fascinated by dinosaurs will probably eagerly absorb knowledge about them no matter how they are taught. However, those with no interest in dinosaurs, but who are *required* to learn about them in school, may benefit from a teaching approach that sparks their interest by incorporating their preferred learning style, such as building three-dimensional models.

Another consideration is that children who excel in only one kind of intelligence or who prefer only one way to learn may be weak in other kinds of thinking and learning. They can benefit from teaching approaches that encourage them to think in ways that activate their *less* preferred learning style. For example, children who are visual learners and who prefer to learn through pictures may benefit from teaching that involves verbal information, because that approach could strengthen their language skills.

Principle 9
Children under eight years benefit more from hands-on learning than from digital educational activities. Furthermore, too much screen time can interfere with the learning process by stifling the imagination, promoting passivity, and replacing valuable playtime.

Many people believe that young children can benefit from educational software or informational videos. However, screen-based activities are neither an effective form of education nor a good form of entertainment for children under eight years of age. Research indicates that excessive screen exposure during early childhood can lead to later attention problems, lower cognitive and social development, poor communication and problem-solving skills, and an increased risk of developing myopia (nearsightedness).

Children learn better through real-life experiences and hands-on toys than by looking at a screen (or even controlling objects on a screen). Spending an hour building with blocks, playing in the snow, or even arguing with siblings provides more learning opportunities and supports better brain development than an hour of screen-based activities, regardless of how educational they are claimed to be.

After eight years of age, children can benefit more from digital educational activities. Online learning opportunities can supplement and reinforce other kinds of learning, but they should never *replace* real-life, tangible experiences and outdoor play.

Principle 10
Children learn best in the absence of tests, grades, rewards, criticism, punishment, or competition.

Giving tests, grades, rewards, criticism, and punishment may lead to temporary compliance and good performance but does not increase children's motivation or result in meaningful learning. On the contrary, those approaches can cause stress and interfere with learning. Even good grades can contribute to children's stress and fear of failure. However, that is not their only negative effect. Studies have shown that good grades and other kinds of rewards can have the opposite effect of what is intended.

A large body of research has found that rewards can undermine learning by reducing intrinsic motivation. The more children want a reward, the more they may dislike whatever they have to do to get it. For example, if children receive rewards for reading books (such as a special treat for each book completed), they may read but only as long as rewards are offered. After the rewards stop, they will be *less inclined* to read books. In fact, they will spend less time reading than children who were never rewarded in the first place.

When children are encouraged to focus on achievement measured by test scores, grades, or class ranking, they stop focusing on what they are learning, and the quality of their learning decreases. If our goal is for children to enjoy learning for its own sake, strive for understanding, and become eager lifelong learners, we must avoid the use of these external "motivators," which are not really motivators at all. Giving grades only motivates children to want good grades, and they will do whatever it takes to accomplish that goal, including cheating. When teachers work with children's natural desire to learn and follow the principles of learning described in this book, children enjoy the learning process and do not need any external motivation.

In addition to these drawbacks of grades, test results don't really indicate how much children have learned. On math tests, for example, a child may arrive at the correct answer by applying memorized calculation procedures without fully understanding the underlying concepts. On the other hand, a child who clearly understands the underlying concepts could receive a low grade due to a simple calculation error. It's unrealistic to think that a single test score or letter grade can provide a meaningful assessment of a child's learning.

There are two primary methods of grading and using tests: norm-referenced testing and criterion-referenced testing. Norm-referenced tests are usually multiple-choice tests, in which children must select the correct answer from three or four options. In this approach, grades are assigned based on a child's performance compared to other children who took the same test. For example, if 100 children take a test, the top ten may receive the highest possible grade, while the bottom ten will receive failing grades. In the United States, standardized norm-referenced multiple-choice tests use percentiles to compare children to each other.

Norm-referenced tests are designed *with the primary goal of rank ordering children.* In fact, if every child answered all the questions correctly, the tests would be considered too easy rather than recognizing that students had mastered the material. These tests *reveal nothing about how much children have learned.* Furthermore, they can cause children with low scores to feel inferior to other children and can lead to unhealthy competition.

However, the major harm occurs when the scores are used to compare schools to each other, a common practice in the United States. Teachers feel pressured to focus on test preparation, such as test-taking skills and memorization of isolated facts. Research has found that this kind of instruction takes valuable time away from more meaningful educational activities. It also causes children to lose interest in learning, results in only short-term memorization, and sacrifices deeper understanding.

In the method known as criterion-referenced testing, grades or scores are assigned based on the number of correct answers. For example, if a math test contains ten problems, a child who misses one receives a score of nine. This approach is much less harmful because it doesn't compare children to each other, and it's even possible for all the children to receive a perfect score. It also provides useful feedback about how much each child has learned and where the child might need help. Additionally, children can track their progress by comparing their performance *to their own past performance.* Unfortunately, however, even criterion-referenced testing can be stressful for some children.

A major problem with all tests that involve clear, simple answers (such as multiple-choice tests) is that they measure only superficial knowledge based on memorization of facts, definitions, or procedures. They cannot measure real learning or the depth of a child's thinking. Oral exams (if conducted in a supportive way) and those requiring essays, written responses, or problem-solving steps can show more evidence of learning but are harder to grade objectively.

We might assume that children attribute good grades to the fact that they have learned something. However, studies suggest otherwise. When children are asked why they received a high grade on a test, they typically give a range of responses. Some might say it's because they studied hard or because they are smart. Others might reply that the test was easy or they were lucky. Very few children attribute good grades to the fact that they have actually *learned* something.

Principle 11
Stress and trauma can interfere with the learning process by causing confusion, anxiety, grief, anger, and difficulty concentrating. The learning process is enhanced when children are allowed to release painful emotions through the natural healing mechanisms of play, laughter, and crying.

Research indicates that children learn best when they feel safe and their lives are free of stress. Children who feel anxious and unsafe cannot concentrate well. Past trauma can also interfere with their ability and motivation to learn. Studies have found that children who have been abused, neglected, or traumatized in other ways often struggle to learn and show cognitive delays compared to other children.

We therefore need to create safe, stress-free learning environments and give children opportunities to heal from trauma. Children are born with the ability to recover from trauma when they feel safe and supported. Their natural healing mechanisms include crying, laughter, and specific types of play in a safe environment with loving adults who support these recovery processes. Healing from trauma in these ways can improve children's ability to concentrate and learn.

Principle 12
Children learn best when they have a warm, supportive relationship with their parents and teachers. The learning process is enhanced when parents and teachers:

• Show acceptance and love while providing quality attention.
• Use encouragement instead of praise, rewards, or criticism.
• Have age-appropriate expectations (neither too high nor too low).
• Use a non-punitive approach to discipline.
• Encourage children to ask questions and be independent thinkers.
• Accept children's painful emotions and allow them to cry.

This principle overlaps with others, but its primary focus is on the importance of loving relationships. Children learn best when they feel emotionally connected to parents and teachers who follow the principles of learning described in this book.

Strong connections are fostered when the adults are accepting, loving, and attentive. Children cannot learn well from people who are cold, critical, judgmental, or punitive; or who tell them to stop crying. Inappropriate expectations can also hinder the learning process.

Additionally, researchers have studied the effects of praise compared to other kinds of encouragement. Contrary to common belief, praise with value judgments, such as the word "good," can lower children's self-esteem and diminish their motivation and performance. In fact, its unwanted consequences are identical to those resulting from the use of grades and rewards (as discussed in principle 10). Children benefit from both feedback and encouragement during the learning process, but it is possible to offer this kind of support while avoiding judgment words. (Suggestions for alternatives to praise are offered in Chapter 5.)

Chapter 9

Trust and Lifelong Learning

> *"There is no end to education. It is not that you read a book,*
> *pass an examination, and finish with education. The*
> *whole of life, from the moment you are born to the*
> *moment you die, is a process of learning."*
> —*Jiddu Krishnamurti*

IN THIS FINAL CHAPTER, I emphasize the importance of
trust, which underlies the principles of learning described in this
book. I also explain how this approach enhances children's ability
not only to learn effectively as children but also to grow into confident and successful adult learners. I conclude with some words of
encouragement and hope.

Trusting children

The approach described in this book is based on connection and
trust. Your connection with your children, along with your trust
in their ability to learn, are the most important factors that will
help them become confident and successful. When optimal conditions for learning are met, you can trust in your children's inherent
desire and ability to learn. They will create meaningful learning
out of their experiences and become competent, joyful, lifelong
learners.

You can convey trust in your children's ability to learn in several
ways. A primary way to trust children is by encouraging them to
follow their interests and allowing them plenty of time for free play.

While leading workshops around the world, I have encountered an assumption in some countries that children must be exposed to stress and hardships early in life so they will be able to cope with stress later in life. This assumption lies at the root of harmful and ineffective teaching methods based on authoritarian control. The mistaken idea is that free play is a waste of time and that future success in school and in life depends on coercion to study and learn from a very young age.

That attitude reveals a fundamental mistrust of children. There is no evidence to support the idea that early school stress is helpful or that children need to form good study habits early in life. On the contrary, considerable evidence suggests that children develop better emotional health when their lives are free of stress and when they have plenty of time to play. In our well-meaning efforts to help children learn and succeed, we mustn't forget to let them be children. This approach to parenting and teaching will strengthen them and help them develop the self-confidence and resilience needed to handle life's later stresses. It will also help them maintain the motivation to learn with which they are born.

You can also show trust by supporting your children's individual learning styles. Children differ in how they like to learn. As explained in Chapter 8, their preferred ways of learning often reflect their strongest kind of intelligence.

Marion Rose described her two children's distinct learning styles:

> As a child, my daughter loved structured learning with workbooks, reading books, handwriting practice, responding to written questions, and going through material in a set order. My son was completely different in how he loved to learn. He didn't enjoy reading books or doing handwriting. Instead, he enjoyed learning in more natural ways in the context of doing what he loved to do. As young adults, they both still love to learn in their own unique ways.

Supporting your children's timing is another way to show trust. Children often spend several days or weeks focusing intently on mastering one skill. During that time, they may show very little interest in other kinds of learning. This behavior is perfectly normal, although it differs considerably from a typical, well-balanced school curriculum that provides daily instruction in each subject.

Marion Rose described her daughter's choice to study a subject that interested her:

> When my daughter was about twelve, she became fascinated by flags. For months, during hours each day, she drew pictures of many of the world's flags. She was homeschooled, so she had plenty of time to do this. She was totally immersed in learning everything about the flags as well as the countries they represented. She absolutely loved the process. Now, ten years later, she still remembers the flags and which countries they belong to.

The following example is a true story about one of my children's classmates in the alternative program that I helped start (described in Chapter 1). It illustrates trust in children's natural learning pace:

> Roger was six years old when his parents enrolled him in the alternative class. He loved sports but showed no interest in academic subjects and resisted learning to read. In the alternative class, the children were allowed to choose their own activities for several hours each day. Roger chose to spend his time practicing handball on the playground. (American handball is a sport in which players take turns using their hands to hit a ball against a wall.) Every day, he could be seen diligently practicing at one of the handball courts, usually alone. In the classroom, the teacher often encouraged him to participate in individual reading instruction, but he always refused. After several months, Roger excelled at handball, began to compete with other

children, and regularly won. Then one day, near the end of the school year (when he was seven years old), he told the teacher that he was ready to read and asked her to teach him. He learned to read within a month.

In this example, Roger focused on perfecting a physical skill before he felt ready to read. He had strong kinesthetic intelligence, and the teacher understood that he needed to excel at something he felt confident in to build up his confidence and self-esteem. It's also possible that he simply wasn't ready to read until the age of seven. When he finally felt ready, he learned effortlessly. *(Please note that children who resist reading or who struggle with reading should be assessed for dyslexia before assuming that they are simply late readers.)*

In the following two examples, a client described how she trusted her son to determine his own process and timing for mastering two physical skills: riding a bicycle and swimming:

On our son's third birthday, we gave him a balance bike (a walking bike without pedals). The first thing he did was look for the pedals, but there weren't any. This showed us that he was interested in a bike with pedals. A few months later, we bought him a small bike with pedals at a flea market. We consciously avoided giving any advice while he learned to ride it. Instead, we offered encouragement and celebrated his progress. It only took him a few hours, and he was riding confidently. Now, as a teenager, he has always been confident on his bike and knows his capabilities. He has never been reckless, even when mountain biking. He assesses the curves and knows if he can handle them. This trust in his learning process allowed him to listen to himself and develop his skills.

We also tried to interfere as little as possible with his swimming progress and trusted him to learn in his own way. He wore swim helpers (floatation aids) for quite some time, longer than most children, but we trusted the process.

One summer, he decided not to wear them anymore and easily swam to the middle of the lake. Now he is a confident swimmer.

Children who have not been trusted to learn may temporarily lose touch with their inherent motivation to learn and experience a decline in self-confidence. This will be especially evident if they have experienced a great deal of direct instruction involving tests, competition, punishments, or rewards before being placed in a learning environment with more freedom and less authoritarian control.

If you switch your children from a traditional school to a more progressive one (or if you begin homeschooling them) you may notice a period of several months during which they appear to lack self-direction and motivation to engage in learning activities. During this initial period of adjustment, children commonly say that they are bored. At the same time, they may strongly resist any activity that resembles traditional schooling. It's important to offer some stimulation but resist the temptation to over-direct your children's activities, because they need time to discover their interests. There is no harm in letting them experience boredom. With your ongoing trust in their inherent desire and ability to learn, your children will regain the passion for learning they were born with and begin exploring topics of interest.

Another aspect of trusting children is avoiding pressure to excel or pursue a specific career. If you feel the urge to pressure your children to excel academically, in sports, or in music, you are not alone. When my children were little, I saw a five-year-old girl playing classical violin music, and I thought it would be lovely if my own children could do that. I read about a 12-year-old boy who already had a university degree, and I wondered if my own children might be capable of such an accomplishment. I heard about a 16-year-old girl who had started her own business and used the profits to support a local animal shelter for stray dogs and cats. I would have been very proud if my children had become music virtuosos, academic geniuses, or business entrepreneurs at a young age. However, I also wondered if pushing them toward excellence in these areas was truly beneficial, and I questioned my motivation. I eventually realized that my desire stemmed from my own need to feel good as a mother and to boost my self-esteem.

While raising my children, I tried to remember that the most important thing was for them to enjoy learning and to explore their own interests so they could discover what they liked and what they were good at. I wanted them to find careers based on their own interests and abilities rather than on my aspirations for them. I knew that this approach would be the only way for them to lead fulfilling lives. I also knew that they might need to learn new things later in life if they switched careers. I avoided pressuring them in any way, and I tried not to influence their career choices.

Aspects of trusting children to learn

- Assume that they want to learn.

- Allow them to follow their interests.

- Let them play.

- Support their learning style.

- Trust their timing.

- Don't pressure them to excel.

- Support their career choice.

Joss Goulden described her initial difficulties in trusting her children's natural learning processes while homeschooling them:

At first, it was hard for me to trust my children's natural learning process. In our culture, there is a lack of trust in the innate wisdom of children. Having been raised without trust myself, it took time for me to build more trust in my children and their learning. I have found these principles of learning to be so helpful to be able to trust and support each of my children's unique learning journeys. I have homeschooled my children and have often seen them deeply exploring topics that interest them. I have observed their intrinsic motivation to learn and to develop competence and skills. For example, my daughter did not enjoy writing and found reading difficult. However, when she was twelve, she wanted to get a job in a local cafe and spent the week before starting work there practicing reading, spelling, and handwriting so she would be able to take orders. I did not have to force or coerce her in any way. Now, at 18, she is a passionate reader who also really enjoys creative writing and journalling. Meaningful, real-life experiences have been the richest learning opportunities for my children. The learning experiences that they have enjoyed the most have been self-initiated and self-directed, with my support in helping them explore in whatever ways they were most called to do. Much of their learning, particularly in the early years, was through play. In learning to value all forms of intelligence and all styles of learning equally, I have been able to support my children to learn how to learn. This means that they have developed a life-long curiosity and love of all different types of learning.

Lifelong learning

Learning doesn't stop when we receive a high school or university diploma. Lifelong learning is not only important for finding jobs; it can also be enjoyable. My mother inspired me by her eagerness to continue learning throughout her entire life. She earned a Master's degree at the age of 42, and she took art classes and learned to paint in her eighties. She also began to write poetry at that age. I learned to play the accordion as an adult (with the help of an instruction book, but without a teacher). I also took Spanish classes when I was in my fifties and learned to speak Spanish.

Other family members have also acquired new skills and knowledge as adults. My husband taught himself to build websites using HTML coding (before the existence of website development software), and he created the first website for the Aware Parenting Institute in 1996. He and his father taught themselves to make stained glass windows and established a successful business together. As an adult, my daughter has studied music theory and songwriting on her own and enjoys composing songs and choral music as a hobby.

Several friends have inspired me with their lifelong learning journeys. I had a friend in Switzerland who had not attended the academic high school but took night classes as an adult and passed the university entrance exams at the age of 35. She enrolled in the university and earned a Master's degree in biology at the age of 40. After that, she enjoyed teaching biology for 25 years to middle school students (12 to 15 years old).

I had another friend with whom I shared an office as a psychology graduate student in California. She had spent twenty years working for a telephone company and raising a child as a single mother before attending a university for the first time at the age of 40. She earned a Ph.D. in psychology and became a university professor at the age of 50.

Children have a lifetime of opportunities to pursue their interests and acquire new skills and knowledge. There is no need to cram all of it into their first 18 or 25 years. If we give them the freedom to explore their interests as children, without pressure, they will have the confidence, motivation, and ability to continue learning as adults and pursue meaningful careers.

We don't know what future careers will look like, which is another reason to prepare children for lifelong learning. Both of my children are computer programmers, and the jobs they have today did not exist when they were born. Furthermore, they have had to learn many new things as adults to keep up with the rapidly changing field of computer science.

I was lucky to have parents who supported my choices, did not pressure me to excel as a child, and enrolled me in a progressive school with no tests, homework, or grades. They recognized the importance of play and encouraged me to follow my interests and develop confidence in myself. Additionally, they did not pressure me to pursue any specific field of study.

As a teenager, I had no idea what I wanted to do as an adult. When I enrolled at the University of Geneva, I chose a program leading to a degree in human biology, which attracted me because it focused primarily on science classes. One of the requirements was to attend all of Piaget's classes and lectures in child development. Piaget's work sparked my interest in developmental psychology, so I decided to pursue that field.

My life has been a continual process of learning new things beyond my formal education, and this has allowed me to find meaningful work. When I became a mother, I started thinking about how to raise children, and I realized that I had some ideas that I hadn't encountered in any parenting books, so I decided to write a book. After my first book was rejected by all the major publishers, I taught myself how to become a self-published author, which included learning to use a computer.

After I published my first book (*The Aware Baby*), I began receiving invitations to give lectures and workshops. I learned to create transparencies for overhead projectors and later to give PowerPoint presentations. Eventually, I learned how to do Zoom presentations so I could continue offering workshops during the Covid pandemic. I am grateful for the education I received as a child, which did not destroy my love of learning and gave me the confidence to continue learning new skills as an adult.

It's clear that positive childhood learning experiences can make it much easier to continue learning and achieving new things as an adult. On the other hand, painful learning experiences can have the opposite effect. If your self-confidence or motivation to learn was damaged by harmful teaching methods as a child, you might still be affected by those experiences.

A client explained how her early painful school experiences interfered with her ability to start certain projects:

> I think that school trauma is still affecting me. I find it difficult to start things because they seem overwhelming. Feelings of "I have to" come to mind. Even though I know they are not real, it is still an ingrained, automatic response. I also have thoughts of "I can't do this" or "It's too much." I have a lot of tension and fear of doing things wrong, not being "good" enough, making mistakes, being judged, punished, laughed at, or not belonging.

Joss Goulden explained how her childhood learning experiences damaged her love of learning and how she regained it with the help of therapy:

> I feel that my lifelong learning journey has been very hindered by my childhood learning experiences. I got very little pleasure from learning as a child or as a young adult at university. I have had so much self-doubt and self-criticism, which has frequently interfered with my willingness and capacity to learn. After receiving therapy to recover from my childhood, I was finally able to feel confident to explore whatever I am called to learn. Knowing now that I won't be assessed or judged, I can find support from experts around me on any topic, and I can relax and enjoy learning. I love the challenge and inspiration I feel now when I explore something new. I am free to dive into whatever I want to learn with excitement and enjoyment.

An important part of encouraging children and supporting them on their learning journey is serving as a role model for the learning process. If you continue to learn new things as an adult, your children might benefit from watching you.

One of my clients described how learning to drive served as a good learning experience for her son as well:

> I earned my driving license when my son was four years old. While I was preparing for the test, he learned all the traffic signs with me, because my husband and I were talking so much about them when we were all in the car. I failed my driving test the first time I took it, but I passed it the second time. My son witnessed my sadness about failing, but he also saw that I did not give up and that I passed it the second time.

Summary and conclusion

The main theme of this book is that children are inherently motivated to learn and will do so eagerly and joyfully when the teaching approach matches their natural ways of learning, which are summarized in twelve research-based principles of learning.

You may find it difficult to implement the ideas in this book if you were not raised with this approach, especially if you had traumatic childhood learning experiences. You will inevitably be reminded of those painful events if your children have similar experiences, and it's only natural to feel sad, angry, impatient, anxious, or powerless when this occurs. However, those same painful memories may also inspire you to offer your children different learning experiences from those to which you were exposed.

You may benefit from emotional support to help process the painful emotions that arise as you raise your children. If you find people to talk with (and cry with), you can release some of those painful emotions and think more clearly about how best to meet your children's needs. The exercises at the end of this book offer suggestions to help you explore your feelings about the learning process, your own childhood, and your children's experiences.

You will find it easier to implement the ideas in this book if you are already raising your children with the Aware Parenting approach. Your efforts to guide their learning will naturally merge with your usual parenting practices. If you are not yet practicing Aware Parenting, you may find my other books helpful for gaining a deeper understanding of this approach.

If you are practicing Aware Parenting and choose to home-school your children, you can create an ideal learning environment at home, which will naturally fit with your parenting style. If your children attend school, there may be a mismatch between your parenting style and the approach used in their educational setting. Even if you avoid the use of punishments, rewards, judgments, and criticisms at home, your children might encounter those harmful approaches at school.

It's important to be aware of the impact of such practices on your children. They need you to be their ally and will benefit from your empathy and acknowledgment that those practices can be stressful for them. Remember, too, that you can always help them recover from any stress or trauma they experience in school. With your support, your children can thrive in any learning environment.

My wish for all children is that they reach their full potential and have a lifetime of enjoyable learning experiences. If you are a parent or teacher, my wish for you is to trust the amazing unfolding of children's intelligence, recognize each child's unique gifts, and value the important work that you do. Remember to appreciate children's natural curiosity and wonder as they explore the world, and don't forget to enjoy your own lifelong learning journey. By trusting and supporting children's natural learning processes, we can all help build a better world.

Exercises for Exploring Emotions about Learning

BY EXPRESSING YOUR memories and emotions related to learning, you will find it easier to support your child's educational journey. These exercises are designed to help you think about your personal learning experiences and explore your feelings about learning. I recommend doing these with a partner and taking turns listening to each other. If you prefer, you may choose to write your thoughts in a journal.

Childhood memories
1. How do you feel after reading this book? Did anything surprise, confuse, or anger you? Did it make you feel guilty in any way?
2. Describe a positive childhood learning experience. What made it enjoyable? Now, describe a negative childhood learning experience. What made it unpleasant?
3. Recall a favorite childhood toy or game. Why was it special to you?
4. Do you remember learning something through play? Describe the experience.
5. Describe your favorite teacher and your least favorite teacher. What did you like or dislike about them?
6. What memories do you have of tests, grades, criticism, competition, and homework?
7. Were you ever punished for making a mistake or not following instructions in school? How did that affect you?

8. Did you ever feel stressed, anxious, or unsafe at school? If so, why?

9. Did you ever experience discrimination in school based on your ethnicity, religion, gender, appearance, behavior, or disability? How did it impact you?

10. Describe a time when you learned something purely for the joy of learning. This could be in school, at home, or elsewhere.

11. How did your parents or teachers help build your confidence? Did they ever do something that damaged your confidence?

12. Did your parents allow you to study what you wanted, or were you pressured to pursue a particular field or career? How did that influence your life and your feelings about learning?

Current feelings

1. How do you feel when you see (or imagine) a classroom where children are sitting quietly at their desks, following instructions?

2. How do you feel when you see (or imagine) a classroom where children move freely and engage in self-directed activities, either alone or in small groups?

3. Do you often feel the urge to correct your child's mistakes?

4. Do you ever feel that your child's play is a waste of time?

5. Are you concerned about your child's future ability to earn a living?

6. How do you feel about your child's current interests?

7. Do you feel tempted to push your child academically, musically, or athletically?

8. Do you feel the urge to steer your child toward a specific career?

9. Do you trust your child's natural learning process? If not, what makes it difficult for you?

10. What are your strengths in supporting your child's learning? In what way would you like to improve?
11. Do you have a child who struggles with learning? How does that make you feel?

If your child attends school

12. How do you feel about your child's school and teachers? Is there anything you dislike or find concerning?
13. How do you feel when your child has a lot of homework?
14. How do you feel when your child receives a high or low grade?
15. Do you feel confident in your ability to support your child emotionally with school-related stress?

If you homeschool your child

16. How do you feel about homeschooling? What aspects are going well? What would you like to change?

Lifelong learning and goals

1. How have your childhood learning experiences affected your desire or ability to learn as an adult?
2. What new knowledge or skills have you acquired as an adult? How do you feel about your achievements?
3. What would you like to learn in the future? How can you achieve this goal, and what might interfere?

Definitions of Terms

Accommodation
Piaget's term referring to children's modification of their mental structures as they assimilate new information.

Alternative schools
Sometimes called "progressive schools" or "open classrooms," this term refers to a variety of schools that differ from most traditional ones by incorporating several of the learning principles described in this book.

Behaviorist learning theory
A theory of learning based on the work of the American psychologist B.F. Skinner. The core idea is that learning consists of specific facts and skills acquired through behavioral reinforcement with rewards. This approach is also known as operant conditioning.

Broken-cookie phenomenon
A term used in Aware Parenting referring to a situation in which a child cries in response to a small incident, with the outburst appearing disproportionate to the event. The minor issue, such as a broken cookie, serves as a pretext for the child to release accumulated stress or tension from a previous traumatic experience.

Constructivism
A theory of learning inspired by the work of the Swiss psychologist, Jean Piaget. It suggests that children play an active role in the learning process by forming theories as they assimilate information.

Criterion-referenced testing
A testing method in which a person's grade or score is based on the number of correct answers, independent of how others perform on the same test.

Developmental spelling
see Invented spelling

Direct instruction
An educational approach in which teachers provide information, and students are expected to learn by listening and observing.

Dissociation
One of two primary physiological reactions to trauma. (The other is hyperarousal.) During dissociation, children become quiet, passive, compliant, inattentive, unresponsive, and numb.

Dyslexia
A neurological learning difference with high heritability, in which children struggle with reading but often excel in other subjects.

Guided discovery
An educational approach in which teachers provide children with experiences, questions, or problems to think about and guide them toward discovering facts and concepts without direct instruction.

Homeschooling
The practice of supporting children's learning at home without sending them to school.

Hyperarousal
One of two primary physiological reactions to trauma. (The other is dissociation.) During hyperarousal, children may become agitated, distractible, impulsive, hypervigilant, defiant, reactive, aggressive, or destructive.

Intrinsic motivation
The desire to do something without external incentives, such as rewards or punishments.

Invented spelling (also called Developmental spelling)
An educational approach in which teachers encourage children to write stories freely, without correcting their spelling.

Learning by discovery
A method in which children discover facts and concepts through their own experiences rather than direct instruction.

Learning style
A child's preferred method of learning, often influenced by their strongest type of intelligence.

Mental structures
Piaget's term referring to organized cognitive frameworks that children develop as they interact with their environment and assimilate information. These structures function like scientific theories, guiding how children perceive the world and solve problems.

Meshing hypothesis
A theory suggesting that children learn best when teaching methods align with their preferred learning styles.

Neurodiversity
A term describing the natural variation in neurological characteristics within the human population. Note: In this book, the term "neurodiverse" is not used to describe individual children, because it implies a permanent neurological deviation from the norm. Some of the conditions for which it is commonly used could be caused by temporary psychological or environmental factors.

Nondirective child-centered play
A type of interactive play in which an adult gives full attention to the child while allowing the child to lead the play.

Nonsense play
A term used in Aware Parenting referring to a type of interactive play that incorporates exaggeration, mistakes, or anything silly and nonsensical.

Norm-referenced testing
A testing method in which a person's grade or score is based on their performance relative to others who took the same test.

Power-reversal play
A term used in Aware Parenting referring to a type of interactive play in which an adult pretends to be stupid, weak, or incompetent, allowing the child to feel smart, powerful, and competent.

Self-determination theory
A theory of motivation suggesting that people are naturally inclined to grow and seek challenges, and that optimal motivation occurs when three fundamental psychological needs are met: autonomy, competence, and relatedness.

Self-directed learning
An approach to education in which students take control of their learning by choosing what and how they learn.

Separation games
A term used in Aware Parenting referring to a type of interactive play that incorporates separation and reunion between the adult and the child, such as hide-and-seek. Separation games can help children cope with separation anxiety.

Stimulation
In the context of learning, stimulation refers to a rich environment providing age-appropriate experiences, toys, books, educational materials, and social interactions.

Symbolic play
A type of play in which children act out scenarios using dolls or other toys to represent real people or things.

Symbolic thought
The understanding that certain symbols (such as words and numbers) represent something beyond themselves. Language and symbolic play both require this cognitive ability.

Theory of multiple intelligences
A theory proposing that intelligence is not a single entity but a collection of distinct abilities and that people differ in their strongest kind of intelligence, such as mathematical, kinesthetic, and visual intelligence.

Appendix: Educational Reformers

THIS APPENDIX includes additional information about the educational reformers in Europe and North America mentioned in Chapter 7. Their names are listed in chronological order according to their birth years. Some of their writings are included in the references of this book.

John Amos Comenius (born in 1592)
A philosopher, educator, and theologian from what is now the Czech Republic. He advocated for universal education (including women and the poor) using pictorial textbooks in modern languages instead of Latin. Considered the father of modern education, his ideas influenced educational reforms in Europe.

Jean-Jacques Rousseau (born in 1712)
A Swiss philosopher who wrote about politics, religion, and education. He argued that children should learn through direct experiences appropriate for their age rather than formal instruction. His work influenced progressive education movements.

Johann Heinrich Pestalozzi (born in 1746)
A Swiss teacher and educational reformer who emphasized teaching the whole children through sensory experiences, emotion, and hands-on activities. He believed in education for all, including the poor, and inspired later reformers like Fröbel.

Friedrich Fröbel (born in 1782)

A German teacher who created the concept of kindergarten and coined the term, which means "children's garden." He studied with the Swiss educator Pestalozzi and believed that early childhood education should be playful, creative, and based on hands-on activities.

Mary Peabody (born in 1806)

An American teacher and educational reformer who wrote about women's rights, promoted universal free education, and helped introduce the kindergarten movement to the United States.

Francis Parker (born in 1837)

An American teacher known as the father of progressive education. He emphasized experiential learning, creativity, and democracy, and his work influenced later progressive educators, including John Dewey.

John Dewey (born in 1859)

An American philosopher, psychologist, and educational reformer who promoted progressive education. He emphasized learning by doing, democracy in education, and critical thinking. His ideas continue to be highly influential in modern education.

Rudolf Steiner (born in 1861)

An Austrian philosopher who founded a spiritual movement called anthroposophy and founded Waldorf education (Steiner schools). His approach to education integrated academics, arts, and practical skills, focusing on imagination and creativity.

Maria Montessori (born in 1870)

An Italian physician and educator who developed a pedagogical approach emphasizing hands-on, self-directed learning, mixed-age classrooms, and specially designed educational materials.

Janusz Korczak (born in 1878)

The pen name of a Polish-Jewish educator, pediatrician, and author whose real name was Henryk Goldszmit. He defended children's rights and ran an orphanage based on respect and democracy for Jewish children in the Warsaw ghetto. When the Nazis invaded the orphanage in 1942, he accompanied the children to an extermination camp and died there with them.

Alexander Sutherland Neill (born in 1883)

A Scottish educator who opposed authoritarian methods in traditional schooling and founded Summerhill School in England, a democratic, student-centered school where children have freedom to make choices about what to learn.

Célestin Freinet (born in 1896)

A French elementary school teacher and educational reformer. He developed a cooperative, student-centered approach to education, emphasizing student choice, projects, and real-life experiences, as well as democratic self-government.

Jean Piaget (born in 1896)

A Swiss developmental psychologist and philosopher known primarily for his theory of cognitive development and his ideas on how children learn. His work has had a major influence on education, giving rise to constructivism, the idea that children are active participants in the learning process rather than passive recipients of information.

Jerome Bruner (born in 1915)

An American researcher in cognitive psychology, learning theory, and education. He developed the concept of the spiral curriculum, in which learners revisit topics at increasing levels of complexity. He emphasized discovery learning and helped found the Head Start movement (a national preschool program for children from low-income families).

John Holt (born in 1923)
An American educator and leading figure in alternative education, particularly homeschooling and unschooling.

David Elkind (born in 1931)
An American child psychologist who studied with Jean Piaget in Switzerland for a year. He is known for his research on play and the impact of stress on children, particularly the pressure placed on them in school.

Daniel Greenberg (born in 1934)
An American physicist who co-founded the Sudbury Valley School and wrote extensively about it, promoting self-directed learning and democratic education.

Eleanor Duckworth (born in 1935)
A Canadian teacher and research psychologist who studied with Jean Piaget in Switzerland. She is known for her research on constructivist learning theories.

Herbert Kohl (born in 1937)
An American educator who wrote about his experiences teaching in underprivileged schools. He promoted progressive education and founded the open school movement in the 1960s.

Howard Gardner (born in 1943)
An American developmental psychologist known primarily for his theory of multiple intelligences.

Peter Gray (born 1944)
An American psychology researcher known for his criticism of traditional schooling and his advocacy for play and self-directed learning. He was a trustee at the Sudbury Valley School.

Thomas Armstrong (born in 1951)

An American educator and author known for his work on multiple intelligences, neurodiversity, and child development.

Alfie Kohn (born in 1957)

An American writer known for his criticism of standardized testing, grades, rewards, homework, and competition.

References

The following research articles and books provide evidence and more information about the twelve principles of learning described in Chapter 8. The full text of these principles (but not these references) is also posted on the Aware Parenting Institute website at the following link: http://www.awareparenting.com/learning.htm.

Principle 1: Innate desire to learn

Di Domenico, S.I. & Ryan, R.M. (2017). The emerging neuroscience of intrinsic motivation: A new frontier in self-determination research. *Frontiers in Human Neuroscience*, 11(145), 1–13.

Holt, J. & Farenga, P. (2017). *How Children Learn* (50th Anniversary Edition). Da Capo Lifelong Books.

Taylor, G., *et al.* (2014). A self-determination theory approach to predicting school achievement over time: The unique role of intrinsic motivation. *Contemporary Educational Psychology, 39*(4), 342–358.

Principle 2: Following children's interests

Baker, S. T., *et al.* (2023). Making space for children's agency with playful learning. *International Journal of Early Years Education, 31*(2), 372–384.

Bandhu, D. *et al.* (2024). Theories of motivation: A comprehensive analysis of human behavior drivers. *Acta Psychologica, 244.*

Conesa, P.J. *et al.* (2022). Basic psychological needs in the classroom: A literature review in elementary and middle school students. *Learning and Motivation, 79* (August), 101819.

Cronin-Golomb, L. M., & Bauer, P. J. (2023). Self-motivated and directed learning across the lifespan. *Acta Psychologica, 232,* 1–15.

Kallick, B. & Zmuda, A. (2017). Orchestrating the move to student-driven learning. *Educational Leadership, 74*(6), 63–57.

Kohn, A. (2006). *The Homework Myth: Why Our Kids Get Too Much of a Bad Thing.* Cambridge, MA: Da Capo Press.

Niemiec, C.P. & Ryan, R.M. (2009). Autonomy, competence, and relatedness in the classroom: Applying self-determination theory to educational practice. *Theory and Research in Education*, 7(2), 133–144.

Patall, E. A. *et al.* (2008). The effects of choice on intrinsic motivation and related outcomes: A meta-analysis of research findings. *Psychological Bulletin, 134*(2), 270–300.

Reeve, J. & Tseng, CM. (2011). Cortisol reactivity to a teacher's motivating style: the biology of being controlled versus supporting autonomy. *Motivation and Emotion, 35*, 63–74.

Principle 3: Learning by discovery

Alfieri, L. *et al.* (2011). Does discovery-based instruction enhance learning? *Journal of Educational Psychology, 103*(1), 1–18.

Allen, A. (2022). An introduction to constructivism: Its theoretical roots and impact on contemporary education. *Journal of Learning Design and Leadership*, Volume 1, Issue 1.

Andrews, J.D.W. (1984). Discovery and expository learning compared: Their effects on independent and dependent students. *The Journal of Educational Research*, 78, 80–89.

Bonawitz, E. *et al.* (2011). The double-edged sword of pedagogy: Instruction limits spontaneous exploration and discovery, *Cognition* 120, 322–330.

Doadu, M.A. *et al.* (2024). Effectiveness of constructivism theory of learning as 21st century method of teaching. *Journal of Advanced Psychology*, Vol. 6(2), 1–11.

Fosnot, C.T. (Ed.) (2005). *Constructivism: Theory, perspectives, and practice*, 2nd edition. New York: Teachers College Press.

Houdé, H. (2011). Functional magnetic resonance imaging study of Piaget's conservation-of-number task in preschool and school-age children: A neo-Piagetian approach. *Journal of Experimental Child Psychology*, 110 (3), 332–346.

Kamii, C. *et al.* (1991). *Early Literacy: A Constructivist Foundation for Whole Language* (Early Childhood Education Series), National Education Association.

Kamii, C. *et al.* (1999). *Young Children Reinvent Arithmetic: Implications of Piaget's Theory, Second Edition* (Early Childhood Education Series), Teachers College Press.

Kasmiana, *et al.* (2020). The application of guided discovery learning model to improve students' concepts understanding. *Journal of Physics: Conference Series* 1460.

Lafay, A. *et al.* (2021). Can manipulatives help students in the third and fifth grades understand the structure of word problems? *Educational Psychology, 41*(9), 1180–1198.

Muthukrishna, N. & Borkowski, J. G. (1995). How learning contexts facilitate strategy transfer. *Applied Cognitive Psychology, 9*(5), 425–446.

Piaget, J. (1965). *The Child's Conception of Number*. W. W. Norton & Company.

Piaget, J. (1973). *To Understand is to Invent: The Future of Education*. New York: Grossman.

Piaget, J. (1997). *The Construction of Reality in the Child*. New York: Free Press.

Piaget, J. (2001). *The Psychology of Intelligence*. Routledge.

Piaget, J. & Inhelder, B. (1972). *The Psychology of the Child*. New York: Basic Books.

Skene, K. *et al.* (2022). Can guidance during play enhance children's learning and development in educational contexts? A systematic review and meta-analysis. *Child Development, 93*(4), 1162–1180.

Solter, A., & Mayer, R. E. (1978). Broader transfer produced by guided discovery of number concepts with preschool children. *Journal of Educational Psychology, 70*(3), 363–371.

Principle 4: Importance of play

Christie, S. (2022). Why play equals learning: comparison as a learning mechanism in play. *Infant and Child Development, 31*(1), 1–8.

Elkind, D. (2007). *The Power of Play: Learning What Comes Naturally*. Da Capo Press.

Fantasia, V., & Nomikou, I. (2022). The intersubjective roots of pretend play. *Rivista Di Psicolinguistica Applicata, 22*(2), 45–60.

Gray, P. (2011). The decline of play and the rise of psychopathology in children and adolescents. *American Journal of Play, 3*(4), 443–463.

Gray, P. (2013). *Free to Learn: Why Releasing the Instinct to Play Will Make our Children Happier, More Self-Reliant, and Better Students for Life*. New York, NY: Basic Books.

Gray, P. (2016). Children's natural ways of educating themselves still work: even for the three Rs. In D.C. Gears & D.B. Berch (eds.), *Evolutionary Perspectives on Child Development and Education* (Chapter 3, pages 67–93). Springer International Publishing Switzerland.

O'Connor, K.J. *et al.* (2016). *Handbook of Play Therapy* (2nd Edition). John Wiley & Sons.

Sim, Z. L., & Xu, F. (2017). Learning higher-order generalizations through free play: evidence from 2- and 3-year-old children. *Developmental Psychology, 53*(4), 642–651.

Solter, A. (2013). *Attachment Play: How to Solve Children's Behavior Problems with Play, Laughter, and Connection.* Shining Star Press.

Weisberg, D.S. *et al.* (2013). Guided play: Where curricular goals meet a playful pedagogy. *Mind, Brain, and Education, 7*(2), 104–112.

Yogman, M. *et al.* (2018). The power of play: A pediatric role in enhancing development in young children. *Pediatrics,* 142(3),

Yu, Y. *et al.* (2018). The theoretical and methodological opportunities afforded by guided play with young children. *Frontiers in Psychology, 9,* Article 1152.

Principle 5: Appropriate stimulation

Bradley, H. *et al.* (2011). Does the quality of stimulation and support in the home environment moderate the effect of early education programs? *Child Development,* 82(6), 2110–2122.

Lancy, D.F. (2024). *Learning Without Lessons: Pedagogy in Indigenous Communities.* Oxford University Press.

McNally, S. *et al.* (2023). Indirect effects of early shared reading and access to books on reading vocabulary in middle childhood. *Scientific Studies of Reading,* 28(1), 42–59.

Pereira, L. *et al.* (2021). Environmental resources, types of toys, and family practices that enhance child cognitive development. *CoDas,* 33(2).

Pitcher, R. (2014). The importance of a creative and stimulating classroom environment. *Education HQ.*

Principle 6: Best kinds of toys

Clavio, J. C. V. & Fajardo, A.C. (2008). Toys as instructional tools in developing problem-solving skills in children. *Education Quarterly,* 66(1), 87–100.

Shodmonova, L., & Panjiyeva, N. (2023). The importance of toys in the development of a child. *Modern Science and Research,* 2(10), 922–925.

Yazgin, E. (2021). Toys and creativity. *Journal for the Education of Gifted Young Scientists,* 9(3), 215–222.

Principle 7: Individual learning rates

Bjorklund, D.F. (2022). *Children's Thinking: Cognitive Development and Individual Differences (7th edition).* SAGE Publications, Inc.

Olson, R.K. *et al.* (2014). Why do children differ in their development of reading and related skills? *Scientific Studies of Reading,* 18(1), 38–54.

Petrill, S.A. *et al.* (2010). Genetic and environmental influences on the growth of early reading skills. *Journal of Child Psychology and Psychiatry*, 51(6), 660–667.

Principle 8: Kinds of intelligence

Armstrong, T. (2000). *In Their Own Way: Discovering and Encouraging Your Child's Multiple Intelligences*. Tarcher/Putnam.

Armstrong, T. (2017). *Multiple Intelligences in the Classroom (4th edition)*. ASCD (Association for Supervision and Curriculum Development).

Felder, R.M. (2010). Are learning styles invalid? (Hint: no!). *On-Course Newsletter*. North Carolina State University (September 27, 2010).

Gardner, H. (2011). *Frames of Mind: The Theory of Multiple Intelligences (3rd edition)*. Basic Books.

Pashler, H. *et al.* (2009). Learning styles: concepts and evidence. *Psychological Sciences in the Public Interest*, Vol. 9(3), 105–119.

Principle 9: Disadvantages of screen time

Christakis, D.A. *et al.* (2004). Early television exposure and subsequent attentional problems in children. *Pediatrics*, 113(4), 708–713.

Hu, B. Y. *et al.* (2020). Relationship between screen time and Chinese children's cognitive and social development. *Journal of Research in Childhood Education, 34*(2), 183–207.

Mallawaarachchi, S. *et al.* (2024). Early childhood screen use contexts and cognitive and psychosocial outcomes: A systematic review and meta-analysis. *JAMA Pediatrics, 178*(10),1017–1026.

Swetha K. (2023). Evaluating the impact of digital screen use on paediatric myopia development: a cross-sectional analysis. *International Journal of Academic Medicine and Pharmacy*, 5(6), 243–246.

Takahashi, I. *et al.* (2023). Screen time at age 1 year and communication and problem-solving developmental delay at 2 and 4 years. *JAMA Pediatrics*, 177(10), 1039–1046.

Principle 10: Disadvantages of tests, grades, punishments, and rewards

Deci, E. L. *et al.* (2001). Extrinsic rewards and intrinsic motivation in education: Reconsidered once again. *Review of Educational Research*, 71, 1–27.

Kohn, A. (1992). *No Contest: The Case Against Competition*. Houghton Mifflin.

Kohn, A. (1999). *The Schools Our Children Deserve: Moving Beyond Traditional Classrooms and "Tougher Standards."* Houghton Mifflin Harcourt.

Kohn, A. (2018). *Punished by Rewards: Twenty-Fifth Anniversary Edition: The Trouble with Gold Stars, Incentive Plans, A's, Praise, and Other Bribes.* HarperOne.

Pulfrey, C., *et al.* (2011). Why grades engender performance-avoidance goals: The mediating role of autonomous motivation. *Journal of Educational Psychology, 103*(3), 683–700.

Robson, D.A. *et al.* (2023). Test anxiety in primary school children: A 20-year systematic review and meta-analysis. *Journal of School Psychology,* 98, 39-60.

Ryan, R. M., & Deci, E. L. (2020). Intrinsic and extrinsic motivation from a self-determination theory perspective: Definitions, theory, practices, and future directions. *Contemporary Educational Psychology,* 61.

Visser, L.N. *et al.* (2022). The association between school corporal punishment and child developmental outcomes: A meta-analytic review. *Children,* 9(3), 383

Principle 11: Impact of stress and trauma

Brown, M.B. *et al.* (2017). Associations between adverse childhood experiences and ADHD diagnosis and severity. *Academic Pediatrics,* 17(4), 349–355.

Mills, R. *et al.* (2011). Child abuse and neglect and cognitive function at 14 years of age: findings from a birth cohort. *Pediatrics,* 127(1), 4–10.

Solter, A. (2022). *Healing Your Traumatized Child: A Parent's Guide to Children's Natural Recovery Processes.* Goleta, CA: Shining Star Press.

Strathears, L. *et al.* (2020). Long-term cognitive, psychological, and health outcomes associated with child abuse and neglect. *Pediatrics,* 146(4).

Thomason, M.E. & Marusak, H.A. (2017). Toward understanding the impact of trauma on the early developing human brain. *Neuroscience,* 342, 55–67.

Yu, J. *et al.* (2024). Patterns of adverse childhood experiences and neurocognitive development. *JAMA Pediatrics,* 178(7), 678–687.

Principle 12: Importance of supportive relationships

Borak, Z. *et al.* (2016). Impact of parenting style on children's academic success. *Journal of Social Sciences and Humanities Research,* 2(2), 1–4.

Bradley, H. *et al.* (2011). Does the quality of stimulation and support in the home environment moderate the effect of early education programs? *Child Development,* 82(6), 2110–2122.

Brummelman, E. *et al.* (2017). When parents' praise inflates, children's self-esteem deflates. *Child Development,* 88(6), 1799–1809.

Furrer, C, & Skinner, E. (2003). Sense of relatedness as a factor in children's academic engagement and performance. *Journal of Educational Psychology,* 95(1), 148–162.

Henderlong, J. & Lepper, M.R. (2002). The effects of praise on children's intrinsic motivation: A review and synthesis. *Psychological Bulletin,* 128(5), 774–795.

Mueller, C.M. & Dweck, C.S. (1998). Praise for intelligence can undermine children's motivation and performance. *Journal of Personality and Social Psychology,* 75(1), 33–52.

Muyarama, K. (2016). Don't aim too high for your kids: Parental over-aspiration undermines students' learning in mathematics. *Journal of Personality and Social Psychology,* Vol. 111(5), 766–779

Pino-Pasternak, D. & Whitebread, D. (2010). The role of parenting in children's self-regulated learning. *Educational Research Review,* 5(3), 220–242.

Rogers, C.R. & Freiberg, H.J. (1994). *Freedom to Learn (Third Edition).* Merrill/Macmillan College Publishing Co.

Solter, A. (1998). *Tears and Tantrums: What to Do When Babies and Children Cry.* Goleta, CA: Shining Star Press.

Solter, A. (2018). *Cooperative and Connected: Helping Children Flourish Without Punishments or Rewards.* Goleta, CA: Shining Star Press.

Topor, D.R. *et al.* (2010). Parent involvement and student academic performance: A multiple mediational analysis. *Journal of Prevention and Intervention in the Community,* 38(3), 183–197.

About the Author

Aletha Solter, Ph.D., is a Swiss/American developmental psychologist, mother of two grown children, international speaker, workshop leader, and consultant. She studied with Dr. Jean Piaget at the University of Geneva, Switzerland, where she earned a Master's degree in human biology. She holds a Ph.D. in psychology from the University of California, Santa Barbara. Her parenting books have been translated into many languages.

Dr. Solter has led workshops for parents and professionals in many countries and is recognized internationally as an expert on attachment, trauma, and non-punitive discipline. She founded the Aware Parenting Institute in 1990 to promote the philosophy of child rearing based on her work. There is a growing list of certified Aware Parenting instructors who are helping to spread this approach around the world.

She is available for lectures, workshops, and private consultations and can be reached at the address below.

The Aware Parenting Institute
P.O. Box 206
Goleta, CA 93116
U.S.A.

Phone & Fax: (805) 968–1868
e-mail: solter@awareparenting.com
website: www.awareparenting.com

What Is Aware Parenting?

AWARE PARENTING IS a philosophy of child rearing based on research in child development. It questions most traditional assumptions about children and proposes a new approach that can significantly improve relationships within a family. Parents who follow this approach raise children who are cooperative, compassionate, competent, nonviolent, and drug free. This philosophy is described in Dr. Aletha Solter's books.

For more information, please visit the Aware Parenting Institute website at www.awareparenting.com.

Aware Parenting consists of the following three elements:

Attachment-style parenting
- Natural childbirth and early bonding
- Plenty of physical contact
- Prolonged breast-feeding
- Prompt responsiveness to crying
- Sensitive attunement

Non-punitive discipline
- No punishments of any kind (including spanking, timeout, and artificial consequences)
- No rewards or bribes
- A search for underlying needs and feelings
- Anger management for parents
- Peaceful conflict resolution (family meetings, mediation, etc.)

Healing from stress and trauma
- Recognition of stress and trauma as primary causes of behavioral and emotional problems
- Emphasis on prevention of stress and trauma
- Recognition of the healing effects of play, laughter, and crying in the context of a loving parent–child relationship
- Respectful, empathic listening and acceptance of children's emotions